DO NOT DESPISE small BEGINNINGS

DO NOT DESPISE small BEGINNINGS

LINDA DEMJEN

ISBN 979-8-9893299-0-8 (paperback)
ISBN 979-8-9893299-1-5 (kindle eBook)

Published by Linda Demjen/A Cup of Cold Water Ministries, Inc.

Book cover design and interior formatting: Crystal L. Barnes, Better Way Publishing LLC

dedication

I would like to dedicate this book to my parents for their many years of putting up with me and all their hard work to raise us in hopes we would go the right way. I am so thankful that my dad and I had a great relationship in his later days, before he left us in 2018, and that my mom is still with us and we have been able to share many wonderful days and years together. I love you Mom and Dad, more than you will ever know.

To my siblings Danny, Donna, Patti, and Susan for all the wonderful times we have had together, good and bad. It's a blessing that we can still love each other in spite of our craziness. Thanks for being there for me and my kids in some very difficult times. I love you all with all my heart.

Especially to my husband Igor, who has ridden the waves of adversity, trials, and joys and sorrows alongside me since 1992. Thank you for always supporting me in everything the Lord has called me to do. I know it hasn't always been easy. You are the best, and my love just keeps growing for you day by day, year by year.

And to my amazing children, Billye and Michael, that have made my life the best it could be. Your love and support have been the best thing I could ever hope for. I am truly blessed to have you for my children and to have the incredible grandchildren you gave me—Theo, Ben, and Ezra; also to my stepson James and his two amazing sons Aiden and Kyle. God gives me exactly what I need in you all. I love you to the moon and back.

First and foremost, I dedicate this book to my Lord and Savior Jesus Christ. Without Him, I could have done nothing that has been accomplished so far and will be in the future of my life. This book is Your book about me and I look forward to You writing my story to the end.

contents

introduction

It is said that in the first six years of your life you are forming
who you will be, but I think God can change anyone and restore anything amiss in our beginning. I am a girl from Kansas, born into a middle-class family in the year 1948. From the
beginning, my dad and mom were hardworking business own-
ers until they struck out on their own, away from parents and
hometown, and Dad became a laborer in construction and then
in the oil fields of Kansas. I remember that he worked long
hours almost six or seven days a week. He was a father who
felt when he provided for his family, he had done his best. In
his later years, the thing he said he missed the most was his
work. He loved to be busy and work with his hands. He was a
master craftsman and builder. Whatever he did, he did it well.
I guess that is where I got my artistic talents and perfection-
ism. I always longed for a close relationship with my dad, but
it didn't seem to happen until the last twenty years of his life.
His long hours of work and a lot of socializing after work in
the local bar or with his buddies stole our time together. Consequently, I grew up not having a close relationship with him.
I suffered from it, because I was always looking for a father
relationship in other relationships with men that were not usually healthy. Not blaming my dad, but aware that in those in-
formative years a parental relationship is very important in
forming who we will be as adults.

Do Not Despise Small Beginnings

My mom worked outside the home or in their joint business ventures from the time of my birth. They both were born of strong German stock; hardworking, honest people. Mom was able to do just about anything to help our family survive. Cooking for five kids day in and day out was a big chore, not to mention cleaning, shopping, school, sports, religious classes, and every other necessity for raising children. It was amazing how she could make a chicken feed seven mouths. What a miracle worker she was. She and dad got to eat the backs, wings, gizzards, and liver, while we five fought over the legs and one breast she had cut into four pieces. While dad hunted, fished, butchered, and gardened, she picked, cleaned, canned, processed, packaged, and froze vegetables and provided for us very well. Our Saturday night ritual was to polish the shoes, take a bath, and get ready for church the next day. We were not rich, but we managed to never go without a meal. Sometimes it was pork and beans or ham and beans, with a fried German dumpling, which I loved and occasionally make today. We didn't know we were lacking in any way.

My mom was a woman of many talents as well. She could do appliance repairs, paint, sew, design clothes, and still keep up with all five of us, even though Dad was not around. She did all the washing with an old wringer washer, bluing for the whites on the stove and a big pot of boiling starch to dip them in. Monday was wash day, Tuesday was ironing day, and I, being the oldest, was quickly inducted into helping with running the clothes through the wringer, hanging them out to dry, sprinkling and getting them ready to iron. I still remember the day my fingers started to go through the electric wringer. That was a wake-up call! Those were the good old days, right?

Introduction

I learned many survival skills from my parents. Most of all to care about others, give my all to whatever I do, have good work ethics, and be honest. All of these things have been an asset to me, as I have gone through many trials in my life that required me to be both mom and dad to my children. After failed marriages, owning a business, being the founder and president of a non-profit, and a minister to the poor and needy in the world, I knew God was watching over me and I was able to take care of myself and my family. Where we begin often prepares us for the destiny God calls us to.

I am grateful for my small beginnings and that my family is still strong and together, even though we had some struggles. I share all this to give you a backdrop to a small piece of the story of my life and to inspire you to not despise your small beginnings. What starts meager and insignificant can become something amazing for the kingdom of God when we let God have the reins of our life. I hope that my story can inspire you to not give up and to see yourself as a beloved child of God that has been created for His purpose and glory.

God truly does make beauty out of ashes. I was lost, a slave to sin, deceived in my mind, living a lie, lied about, lied to, despised, hated, cheated, abused, thrown away, homeless, rejected; yet the Lord Jesus picked me up and turned my life around, put my feet on solid ground, and made something beautiful out of it all. As the old saying goes, it's not how you begin, but how you finish, that counts. I desire to finish well by the grace of God and hear the Lord say, "Well done my good and faithful servant," when He calls me home.

Never stop, keep going!

—Linda

-I-

GOD'S TIMING IS PERFECT

"The Lord God Almighty has His hand on you."

These are the words I saw written on the wall, from the ceiling to the floor, in my dream. There is no greater assurance than knowing that God has not forgotten me, and His hand is upon me. Doesn't everyone want to know this is a promise from Him? Hebrews 13:5 tells us that Father God, our Creator, never leaves us or forsakes us.

"I will uphold you with my righteous right hand"
(Is. 41:10b NKJV).

August 23, 2008, I had fallen asleep in the afternoon, not expecting that the Lord would give me such a profound dream. In the dream I saw myself walking into a house; an ordinary house made of wood, with wooden floors. After I entered the house, I found myself in a hallway, and when I looked to my left I saw my husband, Igor, standing in a doorway. It felt like it was my house. Then I looked to the right and saw my deceased grandma, Julia, walking towards me. I was so surprised to see her. She looked exactly like the grandma I loved so much from my childhood. She smiled when she saw me, and

1

then she hugged me so tight I could hardly stand up. I felt such a deep love from her; the same love I have experienced from the Lord in times past.

While we were in this wonderful embrace, we swayed back and forth in the hallway. I was struggling to find my balance, so I fixed my eyes immediately on the walls in the hallway and noticed they were covered with faint writing. The words were not clear until I scanned down to what looked like the bottom of a long column of sentences. Then I clearly saw the words, *"The Lord God Almighty has His hand on you."* As I moved my eyes back up the wall, I could see that these words were repeated over and over. I wept when I felt the love of God envelope me in the midst of my grandma's hug. There is no greater love than the love of the Lord God Almighty for His children. He gave His only Son as a sacrifice for us, and His love has been proven as we can read in John 3:16. When we become children of God through faith in Jesus, we have access to His love continually. The Word shows us this in John 2:12.

One way we know God's love for us is by how He works in and through our lives. Everything that God does is in His perfect timing. He gave me the dream on that day, at that very hour, because He knew a friend would call me and be struggling with knowing that God loved her. Only thirty minutes after waking from that dream, she called me and was very distressed. She was in a tremendous struggle in her life, questioning whether God had given up on her and did not love her.

We talked, and the Holy Spirit prompted me to share my dream with her. She broke into tears with the complete understanding that He loved her so much He gave me this dream so that she could call me exactly when she needed to hear that God loved her.

The Lord does not sleep (Ps. 121:4). He knows every struggle we go through and exactly what we need at every moment of our existence. This small incidence made a vast difference in my friend's life because she was reassured at that moment of God's love for her. God does not want any of us to ever doubt His love for us, which is why He sent His only begotten Son, Jesus Christ, to reassure us all of His magnificent love for us.

None of us should ever doubt that our Father God loves us. John 15:13 tells us that no one has greater love [no one has shown stronger affection] than to lay down [give up] his own life for his friends. This is what Jesus did for all of mankind. If you don't know how much God loves you, you need to realize it now. The cross is the most profound symbol of His love ever given to mankind.

God gave me a reminder of this one Saturday morning in our prayer room. We were soaking in God's presence, as we love to do, when I received a vision of the cross on a hill. Jesus wasn't on it, but a great brilliant light burst from it in all directions, and the Lord spoke to my heart—"My people don't know what I did for them on the cross." It made me realize that many Christians are not really living with the understanding of how much God loves them. We can know about what God did for us, but do we really know or understand the significance of what He did on that cross for us?

To know in Greek is the word *ginosko*, which means recognition of truth by personal experience. In Hebrew it is yada, which means to perceive or be acquainted with. When we experience God's love through a life experience, such as my friend did, we can truly know and understand that He loves us so much that He gave His life for us. This has been the process of my life since first receiving Jesus as my Lord and Savior in 1991. This is the love of God, as Jesus demonstrated, when He went to the cross and laid His life down for all mankind. He called his followers friends. He wants an intimate relationship with all His children.

God manifests His love in so many ways in our lives; sometimes we are not even aware of it. In this book, I would like to share some of the ways that God has manifested His love in my life, and perhaps you can begin to see how much God loves you by looking at your own life as I paint a small portrait of my small beginnings with the Lord that led me to where I am today. Be encouraged. He is not finished with you yet!

YOUR NOW IS NOT YOUR FINISH

"For who has despised the day of small things"
(Zechariah 4:10a).

As I said earlier, God's timing is paramount. He knows the precise time you need to go through a trial and the precise time it is completed. Even though we know there is no time in Heaven, God speaks much in His Word about time. The word *time* is used in 563 verses in the Bible. It took God seven days to create the heavens and earth and all things on it, including the first man and woman. He created day and night, the timing of the universes and how it functions, the stars, the sun and moon and their rising and setting, the tides in the ocean, the changing seasons, the timing of every movement of the earth and everything on it. I have heard it said that God has assigned angels to keep the planets in orbit. A second of change off-course could destroy everything.

In the book of Genesis, the first two chapters tell us the number of days it took God to create everything in the heavens and the earth. If time was important enough for God to mention the number of days it took Him to create everything, why wouldn't time still be an important part of our existence?

Our very lives revolve around the clock; we all live on a time schedule, even to our own demise. We sleep when the sun goes down and get up when it rises if our inner clock is working correctly. God created the day and night; He knew we needed to work and to rest as He did on the seventh day of creation (Gen. 2:1, 2). God created time, and He had an excellent reason for it. Time should never become another problem for us. We are to be good stewards with it and realize that, if something doesn't go the way we think it should and when it should, we have perhaps unknowingly stepped out of God's plan. His timing is always perfect. God's time differs greatly from the time we live by. Scripture tells us that to God a day is as a thousand years and a thousand years is as a day (2 Pet. 3:8). Praise God there is no time in heaven, but while we are here God uses it for our good.

As I have learned in my life, God was in it all along; it just took me some time to discover what He was up to. Maybe you have a small inkling of what God has called you to do in your life, but you don't know for sure yet, or you don't know at all. I can tell you everything is right on time...just as it is. Even when we go the wrong way and get off track, God is still there, He is still working, He will steer you back if you just look at Him and not your circumstance.

Your *now* is not your *finish*; it's not your end. Keep going. Don't give up and keep your eyes on Jesus. The Holy Spirit often reminds me of this, because life can get very distracting and trying with so many trials and difficulties. There is nothing we can do at times but call out to Him for help, as I did when I first met Him.

-3-

TIME TO MEET JESUS

Psalm 23:4 (NKJV) says it so well:

> *"Yea, though I walk through the valley of the shadow of death, I will fear no evil, for You are with me; Your rod and Your staff, they comfort me."*

We walk through the valley of the shadow of death; we don't stay in the middle of it. It is just a shadow that comes and goes, with the sun's rising and setting. The truth is, while we are walking through it, the Lord God Almighty has His hand upon us. Therefore, we have nothing to fear; not death, pain, sickness, loss of loved ones, financial disaster or wars—no evil will be able to take us down. "In His hand is the life of every living thing and the breath of all mankind" (Job 12:10 NKJV). You see, even when we leave this body, we still live, and if we know Jesus as our Savior, we will live with Him in Heaven eternally. So, death has lost its hold on us and fear has no place in us either. Those who do not know Jesus as Lord and Savior are the only ones that should fear their eternal future. Only with Him is it secure.

I have been through that valley of the shadow of death so

7

many times, as I am sure many of you have, but God has always taken me through it just as He promises to all His children. One of my most difficult experiences took place in Eastern Europe. Shortly after communism had fallen, my husband Igor heard from his mother, who still lived in the former communist country of Czechoslovakia. She was imploring him with letters and phone calls to come and claim back the land that was taken from his grandfather during communism. The Czechoslovak government was giving back or granting restitution to the people all that the Russians had stolen from them during the forty-year occupation of communism. Igor's grandfather was a wealthy landowner. As their rightful inheritance, his mother wanted to give him and his brother their portion of the property that had been taken. Even though it sounded like a great blessing, little did we know it would require four and a half years of very difficult, discouraging, and life-threatening work on our part to accomplish it. This was a valley of trials and tests of our faith that changed us and prepared us for our destiny. We had no idea to what extent the trials would be until we got into the daily grind of going to office after office, dealing with a very broken post-communist system.

Communism fell in Russia on the fateful day of November 9, 1989, when the East Berlin Wall began to be torn down. Both the East and the West Germans began to run to the other side, which led to tearing down that dreadful wall that symbolized oppression for so many years. It started a snowball effect causing the freedom from Communism in Czechoslovakia, Poland, and Hungary, all the Eastern Block. We entered this broken country shortly after.

Let me lay the foundation of my life and the events leading

up to our coming to Czechoslovakia. At the time that Communism was falling, I was about to give birth to my amazing son, Michael, in Tucson, Arizona, who was born on December 19, 1989. All of this is very significant, because again God's timing is everything. He knows the number of the days of our lives, the hour of every event of significance in our lives. Not only that, the Spirit interconnects everything, and in time with the book that is written about us in heaven (Ps. 139:16).

In the few years between my son's birth and the Berlin Wall falling down, I moved from Arizona to New York, thinking that it was a stop for me to go on to West Germany to stay with a friend. As hard as I tried, I could never seem to get the airplane ticket; something always blocked it. Was that God's way of stopping me? Looking back, I am positive it was. Sometimes we just have to admit that God has another plan that was much better, even though it is not visible to us yet. At that time, I did not know Jesus as my Savior, nor did I have a clue that my life was in God's hands regardless of where I was or that I had a calling on my life. In His time and His way, I would find out what that calling was.

It was all a set-up. One day, when I was at the bottom of the pit like Joseph, the son of Jacob (Gen. 37:20-24), I walked into a church in Monroe, N.Y. and knelt down. I called out to Jesus to help me. I said only four words, "Please Jesus, help me!" He answered me immediately, and I heard His still, small voice in my left ear, as though He was sitting right next to me. These are the words I heard clearly: "You have gone astray, now you have come back, I never left you. Take my hand and I will take you through everything." There was His hand again. All I had to do was take hold of it and He would guide me. I didn't have a clue who Jesus really was, or what He had in store for me, but I was going to find out.

If I just look at that one sentence He said to me, I can preach a message. Number one, if I called out to Jesus, then it must be Him that was speaking to me. He knew everything about me before I cried out to Him and where I was at that very moment. He made it clear to me He was there all the time, and if I would trust in Him and fully give myself to Him, He would lead me on the path to everything I needed in my life. I can look back and say, "Wow! The Lord God Almighty has His hand on me." I can add to that He has His hand on you too.

After hearing His voice, I got up and walked out of the church. I was the only human being there, but there was obviously someone much greater and all-knowing than me with me. I went to the back of the church and picked up a church bulletin and took it home with me. Our home was a studio apartment with one room—bathroom and small kitchenette; a mattress on the floor; a table and a few chairs; a television and our clothes. That was it. Things were very bad for us. I couldn't find a job, and my son's father had no job and couldn't find one. Consequently, we couldn't pay our rent, and we had no food in the cupboards or refrigerator. I was living the nursery rhyme, "Old Mother Hubbard, went to the cupboard, to give the poor dog a bone; when she came there, the cupboard was bare, and so the poor dog had none." Even though it seemed like the end in many ways, it was really just the beginning.

I was in the bottom of the pit of despair and hopelessness had set in, which is where God allowed me to get to in my life through wrong choices, disobedience, sinfulness, and literally coming to the end of myself. Did He try to stop me from going this far down? Of course, but my pride and selfishness would not allow me to submit. The things I had filled my mind with and exposed myself to throughout life were directing my choices and led me to the pit of despair. No one made me do the things I did, I was fully to blame, yet I was about to become friends with a merciful and forgiving Savior that had a love for me that no one else could ever match.

Later that night I looked at the church bulletin I had picked up and found an article about a food bank, so I called the number. When you have nothing to eat and no money, you do what you have to for survival, especially if you have a child to care for. You have to understand this was very humiliating for me. I had never wanted to ask anyone for help, since I was always able to help myself, but now I had entered another place in my life I was not familiar with; brokenness, financial ruin, relationship ruin, emotional ruin; my heart and life needed a complete overhaul. Because God loved me and had a great plan for my life, the answer had come, but I didn't know it yet.

The man from the food bank on the other end of the phone apologized that he couldn't bring us food right away, but said he could bring what we needed in the morning. As I went to sleep, I wondered how all this would play out, never having been in this place before. The next morning at 10 a.m., sure enough there was a knock at the door and when I saw the station wagon backed up to our door filled with groceries, I was overwhelmed and couldn't help but shed some tears of gratitude and humility. All the time I was just trying to survive another day and take care of my son and out of the blue a gift from God came to my door.

Miracles do happen! In less than twenty-four hours, our cupboards and refrigerator were full. No more going out in the early morning in the snow to look for soda cans to turn in at the supermarket for five cents each to feed my son. Yes, I had been lowered to survival in a way I would have never expected in my life. The good news was there was a food bank around the corner at another church that we could go to receive food every two weeks, with no questions asked. This experience birthed compassion in me for those who are hungry and need help. Jesus spoke about feeding the hungry, as doing it unto Him. Thank God for churches and food banks that help people in time of need. The Bible says those who do this were the righteous, who would be saved in the final judgment, and the unrighteous, who did not give food to the hungry, will suffer eternal punishment (Matt. 25:31-46). We should have the same love and compassion for those in need as Jesus had for us in our lost and sinful state, when He died and suffered for us on the cross. Jesus was becoming real to me, and I began to know and understand that He was with me.

Looking back, mysterious things were already happening in my life. A most significant sign of God's care for us occurred while I was walking one cold wintery New York morning looking for soda cans, pushing my son in the stroller. I was strolling through a parking lot close to the supermarket, distressed, discouraged and cold, with a north wind blowing and snow still on the ground. I was wondering how I was going to buy food for my son that day, when I looked to my left and saw a twenty-dollar bill plastered in the snowbank. I looked at it for a bit and couldn't believe it was real money. I finally picked it up, and sure enough it was a good old American twenty-dollar bill! I looked all around to see if someone had dropped it in the parking lot and the wind had blown it into that snow bank, but it was Sunday, and the parking lot was totally empty. Then it occurred to me, this must be mine. The Lord God Almighty certainly had his hand on me, even though I did not have a clue.

I was only a short distance from the supermarket where I often went to sell soda cans. It was a relief that I didn't have to sell cans this time to buy groceries. It was so demeaning. Sometimes I would even turn in smashed cans, which was not their usual policy to take, but out of the kindness of their hearts they took them anyway. If I had known how to do a hallelujah dance then, I would have done it all the way to the store. I couldn't understand that this was not luck, but the hand of God working in my life, leading and drawing me to Him. He is always with us. If we could turn around and see Him, we would run smack into Him. He's that close.

Years later, after many years of walking with God, I encountered Jesus literally face to face. I remember one night I laid down to sleep, but was unable to sleep. Tossing and turning in bed at 1:30 a.m., suddenly I saw the face of Jesus. It was so close to mine that I could only see Him out of the corner of my eye. He spoke to me, *"Linda, why are you disturbed, I am here, I will guide you, I will solve these problems, trust Me."* He is so beautiful and magnificent, when He becomes real and close to you. Tears of joy began to flow down my cheeks as I experienced His love for me. What a relief I felt after that and went to sleep immediately. If only we could remember that in the middle of our trials and distresses, it would fill our life with so much more peace. We can sing and dance just knowing that we can lean on His everlasting arms!

-4-

GOD STILL DOES MIRACLES

I had kept a Bible that one of my employees had given me years ago and several other books, so I began to read the Bible every morning in the quiet hours, and I kept hearing that same voice I heard in the church speak to me. Strangely enough it answered every question I had about what I read. It was a precious time, just like it had happened yesterday in my mind. I was being drawn by the Father to Jesus and instructed by the Holy Spirit.

"No one can come to Me unless the Father who sent Me draws him; and I will raise him up at the last day" (John 6:44 NKJV).

The groceries were only the first miracle that happened. Shortly after I encountered Jesus in that church, I received a phone call and a man that I had met once at a meeting offered me a job. He said he would come and pick me up and I could bring my son, since I didn't have a car or a way to have child care. It was amazing. There was a small catch though; he was a former preacher that was leading many people astray with false teachings taken from a set of books popular at this time.

I happened to have these books, which I had studied before I met Jesus personally. He had meetings at his house, which I had attended a few times. The book spoke about Jesus, but it also said that there were many ways to God, and Jesus was just one of them. The one saving grace was that the name of Jesus became known to me again, having not been in church for twenty-five years, and God can use anything to lead us to Him. He used these books to plant the name of Jesus to my mind. I said the name of Jesus that fateful day in the church, and He immediately answered and revealed to me He was always there and never left me. The Bible affirms this as truth in Deuteronomy 31:6 and Hebrews 13:5. The Helper, the Holy Spirit, was guiding me and giving me direction in my broken life, leading me to the only answer, who is Jesus Christ. The more I read the Bible, I began to understand that I was encountering Jesus and the Holy Spirit. Then I realized that the voice I heard in the church was Jesus, and He was still speaking to me as I read His word, and He didn't stop doing miracles.

Shortly after I got the first job, a Jewish man that I met at the Course in Miracles group helped me get another job at a youth shelter. Out of the kindness of his heart he came twenty-five miles to pick me up and take me to my job, where I worked the night shift. His kindness was amazing, as he would also pick me up and take me home in the morning. God's lovingkindness was there for me, every step of the way. He uses people to do His work and He used this man to show me the goodness and mercy of God towards me.

I had a hard time accepting all this help, so I decided I should get my own car. There was no possible way for me to get a car without a loan. I determined that this kind Jewish man was the only person that might be willing to help me. I was ready to ask him for a loan; after all I could pay him back, since I had two jobs now. Needless to say, I was terrified to ask him for help, after all he had already done to help me. I really did not think I deserved it; there was a lot of shame and guilt in my life yet. After rehearsing my speech over and over, the day had come to ask for his help. My plan was to do it when he picked me up to take me to work. My nerves were a mess. I rehearsed and rehearsed what I would say to him. I was sick to my stomach and my palms were sweating when he picked me up. I got in the car dreading what I was about to do and then, God stepped in again. We got two blocks from my apartment and just as I was ready to open my mouth and take a leap of faith to ask him this dreaded question, he said, "My wife and I are going to get a new car and we would like for you to have this car." I almost screamed I was so flabbergasted. Needless to say, I couldn't believe my ears. Now I could say, God is so good! That car was a blessing. It worked perfectly, because he took excellent care of it. I used it for four years, until I no longer needed it. He even took me to get my New York driver's license and insurance for the car. Jesus knows our every need, and He always takes the best care of His children. To some people this may not be considered a miracle. Nevertheless, the Bible says that every good and perfect gift comes down from above, from the Father of lights (James 1:17), so I consider this a very good and perfect gift and it came straight from my Father in heaven to me. If I could have done a high-five with Jesus, this would have been the time.

-5-

GOD PICKED MY MATE

My Abba Father had many other blessings in store for me, but not without trials. While I still remained in Monroe, New York, shortly after in 1991 I met my husband, Igor, who had lived in New York since 1967. We met at the same meeting where I had met the Jewish man; in fact, he brought Igor to the meeting because they both worked at the same prison.

Igor did theater workshops with prisoners that were considered to be criminally insane, such as mass murderers. It was Igor that said something profound at the meeting that drew me to him. He boldly declared that what these people were teaching was false and they were in danger of hellfire; he didn't mince words. I had a check in my spirit after that and talked to him after the meeting and told him I agreed.

Igor and I started our friendship and met a few times again at the meeting and then one day he rode his bicycle to my apartment twenty-five miles to hang out with me and my son. Because I was having a struggle paying my rent and Michael's father had moved out, Igor wanted to help me find an apartment closer to my job in Middletown, where he lived. As it turned out, I couldn't afford anything I saw, so he offered me a place in his enormous 6,000 sq. ft. loft/studio for free, since I could not afford to stay where I was living at the time. Both of us were artists; naturally in my mind it made perfect sense for me to live there. Not to mention, I really kind of liked this crazy Czechoslovakian guy. There was plenty of space for two artists and a small boy and all the baggage we both brought to our relationship. I will also add that we were not mature believers and made a wrong decision by moving in together unmarried.

Even when we make bad decisions, God can make good things out of our mistakes. It was living with Igor that made it clear to me that I was having an encounter with Jesus. He was a Jesus believing Christian, who read the Bible and prayed every day. We began to read the Bible and pray together every day and discuss the scriptures often. This was totally new for me.

After growing up in Communism, where God was considered dead, Igor found Jesus in New York, while having long debates with the wife of a man that was leader of the Full Gospel Businessmen. Igor was a follower of philosophers and intellects and was an artist without God, but a lot of head knowledge. He had spent years of studying and debating with other intellects. His heritage was that of intellects and scientists, as well. His father was one of the first plastic surgeons in the world; he actually studied with Sir Harold Gillis, one of the founders of plastic surgery at Oxford University. Igor's mother was also a very intelligent woman with a degree in linguistics, who founded and maintained the medical library in Bratislava, Czechoslovakia.

While living in Briar Cliff Manor in New York, Igor went

to a certain place daily called the wilderness, to walk and meditate on philosophy, appropriately carrying a book with him. There he encountered a woman on horseback named Eloise Pierce, who began to speak to him and debate with him about Jesus. She was not going to give up on Igor and continued even in frustration to try to get him to see the truth through all that philosophical mumbo jumbo. I am sure she had all the Full Gospel Business group praying for this hardheaded intellectual Slovak. Finally, one day she said with authority to him, "Get in that gardener's shed and ask Jesus to show you who He is." He somehow managed to be obedient in his high-mindedness and did exactly that. When he asked Jesus who He was, he heard in his mind these words, "If you want to know Me, you will have to forget everything you know and let me teach you." His immediate thoughts were, how dare you tell me this, do you know how much I have studied and how much I know? In spite of that his spirit said, "Yes, Lord."

From there he threw away all his intellectual books and got a Bible. In fact, he still had an Amplified Bible that Mrs. Eloise gave him, when I met him twenty-five years later. She even made a trip to Czechoslovakia to meet with his mother years later to tell her about her son's born again experience.

Igor started attending the Full Gospel meetings with Mrs. Eloise, who lead him to Jesus and her husband Charles, who was the leader of the meetings. This group of Spirit-filled believers gathered together in hotels or rooms where they would just meet to seek Jesus and wait for the Holy Spirit to move. They were called the Full Gospel Business Men. He saw the move of God with many miracles and was filled with the Holy Spirit through this ministry and was changed completely.

At that time, He was involved in a world-famous theater group led by Robert Wilson, where he helped write and create the music for the productions. They traveled the world and performed, so he was famous, and I might add very full of himself, but the Lord was about to end all that and humble him and bring him into another place for His purpose. After meeting Jesus, when he went back to his theater group and declared that he was a Christian and Jesus was the only way, everyone began to detest and fight against him and his new life.

Our new life in Christ means a change and especially in the people we hang out with.

2 Corinthians 5:17 says we are new creatures in Christ, and the old has passed away. It means walking in a whole new life, and change has to happen. It is the evidence of our conversion. We often don't even look the same. The sanctification process begins and transformation is ongoing from that point throughout our days on earth. The calling to walk with God was in motion for both Igor and I and God had brought us together for a purpose that we could not see at the time, but in the years to come we would be amazed at what He could and would do through us and in us.

God knows who we should be with in this life. I had tried it several times before and failed with my own choices. My advice to single people is to wait on the Lord's choice for you and you will save yourself a lot of trouble.

-6-

SANCTIFICATION THROUGH TRIALS

After coming to Christ, if you have made a true commitment to follow Jesus, every person must go through sanctification. The Biblical meaning of "sanctification" is *the process of separating ourselves from the profane things of this world*, of consecrating and dedicating ourselves to God, and then of purifying ourselves from sin through repentance and renunciation to renew our soul and cleanse our spirit. To be sanctified is to be set apart for the Lord. A perfect example of this in the Bible is the story of Jeremiah the prophet. He heard from the Lord, "Before you were born I sanctified you" (Jeremiah 1:5 NKJV). God had already set him apart to be a prophet, even before he was in his mother's womb. What did God set you apart for?

The Bible says everything about you is written in a book. "Your eyes saw my substance, being yet unformed. And in Your book they all were written, the days fashioned for me, when as yet there were none of them" (Psalm 139:16 NKJV). I love what The Passion Translation says in this verse, "You saw who you created me to be before I became me! Before I had even seen the light of day, the number of days you planned for me were already recorded in your book."

Isn't it wonderful to know God knows and has a plan for your life. His desire is for the book about you to be fulfilled. We have to let Him help us walk it out, so He can keep turning the pages all the way to the end.

During this time of post conversion, I was being transformed and rid of many demons from my past. Believe me, I needed deliverance from them, so there were many battles in mine and Igor's relationship in the beginning. I spent fifteen years involved in the New Age beliefs and practices of all kinds of false ways of seeking false gods. I was highly deceived and led astray from the truth. The closer I drew to the true and living God, Jesus Christ, the harder the fight got. It is just as Paul said, we have to war against the flesh in the Spirit and we are not wrestling against flesh and blood, but principalities and powers and rulers of darkness and spiritual hosts of wickedness in the heavenly places (Eph. 6:12). I was in the middle of an all-out war for my soul but the Lord was on my side and I would not lose!

Maybe you have just met Jesus and even confessed Him as your Savior, then it seemed like everything around you began to fall apart. I will say to you, this is not a bad thing but a part of the sanctification process that must take place in your life, in order for you to reach a deeper relationship with Jesus and fulfill your divine purpose here on earth. What was written in the book in heaven about you, before you were in your mother's womb, can only be fulfilled by going through the sanctification of your flesh, mind, and will.

The blood of Jesus covers every sin. There were many

things in my past I was ashamed of, and day by day the Holy Spirit was bringing conviction of my sin to my spirit and leading me to the truth, just as Jesus spoke to the disciples before His death (John 16:8,13).

I was confused and didn't know what I believed for sure yet, but as I kept reading the Word of God, I was beginning to understand who God was and how that played an important part in my life. The fight for my soul was in full force, as I began to understand that God was there for me and Jesus was the answer for my life. I began to confess Jesus as my Savior, not really understanding fully, but the name of Jesus is so powerful that His name alone, His Word and His blood shed for us that completed His work on the cross was working in my life in spite of my lack of understanding.

This might be a testimony that you can relate to or not, but just know that Jesus is calling you closer to Him in every circumstance of your life. What looks like a disaster is really a blessing in disguise. Paul spoke about us not understanding what is happening now, as we go through trials, but that in time we would. I understand now what I didn't then, and all the struggles and trials that made me want to give up and run away at the time they were happening, make complete sense now. It was all for my good. The Apostle Paul's letter to the Romans says, "And we know that all things work together for good to those who love God, to those who are the called according to His purpose" (Rom. 8:28 NKJV). This scripture eventually became life to me after many hard and life threatening experiences.

Now that Igor and I were living in the same house, it wasn't long before Igor and I were calling ourselves husband

and wife, and we decided to stand in front of God and repeated our marriage vows to each other. We had our own private marriage ceremony. I don't know if I was naïve or I was justifying my sin in my own mind, but being a brand new Christian and knowing nothing, I thought that was a great thing to do. After broken trust, abuse, and abandonment in previous relationships and marriages, I was not eager to get married again. To Igor, it was the best way to marry, because it was before God, not man. Later on, we realized our error and after repentance, by His grace we were redeemed and forgiven. I love the way the Lord corrects us and disciplines us for our good, even though it is painful sometimes.

> *"For the flesh lusts against the Spirit, and the Spirit against the flesh; and these are contrary to one another, so that you do not do the things that you wish" (Gal. 5:17 NKJV).*

God takes us on adventures in this life, in the spirit. Our flesh is constantly warring against it, but with a little bit of faith and trust in the Lord and a lot of grace, we can make it through. Our desire is to do the right thing, and yet sometimes we still fail, which is why we need the grace of God to cover our sins. Some habits die slowly, some He delivers us from instantly. We cannot run or hide from God. He is always going to find us and bring us face to face with our sin so He can deliver us from it. He will use every circumstance to make us better, draw us closer and make us more like Him. His word says, if we draw near to Him, He will draw near to us (James 4:8). Then we can begin to allow Him to strip away the veil that covers our understanding and put to death the old sin nature that Christ died for. We are new creatures in Christ; the old life has passed away, and sometimes it feels like He uses a hammer and a chisel to slowly chip away the old habits, friendships, addictions, lusts and desires, sins, failures, and shame from our past life (2 Cor. 5:17). My son said to me recently that it is like there are leaky pipes that need to be tightened and the Father is constantly tightening and tweaking us and making us more usable for Him. His ultimate goal is to see His glory revealed in us and through us. Don't lose heart, hold on, the Lord God Almighty has His hand upon you and never leaves you or forsakes you.

As I advanced in this new life in Christ, the past receded further and further from me and the things I used to do and like were no longer there. It is finished! I am not the person I was when I began my walk with God, even though my name is still the same, my hometown is still the same, my family is still the same. There are a multitude of visible differences in my lifestyle, my thinking, my desires, my words, my deeds; all things are new in Christ.

-7-

ENTERING THE LAND OF DESPAIR

We don't know our destiny, but we are given clues and desires in our heart by God, designed to lead us to it. It's been my experience that it usually doesn't make sense to us as we are living it. The Lord continually offers us pieces to the puzzle of our life; it's up to us to fit them in the right place through our choices, words, actions, and most of all submission to Him and our prayers for His guidance. Proverbs 3:5,6 NKJV says, "Trust in the LORD with all your heart, and lean not on your own understanding; In all your ways acknowledge Him, and He shall direct your paths." The key is to let God have the reins of your life and let Him direct your steps. Usually, your destiny will end up being something you never would have believed or ever thought of. I can certainly say that about my life as a missionary and world traveler.

God directed our path to Czechoslovakia for the first time in 1993 for a month-long stay with Igor's mother to assess the prospect of helping her retrieve the property of her father. We found gray crumbling buildings all around us, and more than that a Godless nation and people who had been brainwashed and tormented into wrong thinking for forty years. It was a mindset that could not be changed to the truth easily, except with the Holy Spirit's power and God's mercy and grace. After the Berlin Wall came down, the churches of America and other Christian nations quickly entered to share the gospel. Evangelism was an open door, and many were hungry for God. Those who had attempted to keep their faith returned to the church openly, and those who were still alive and in prison for their faith were released. God only knows how many were killed for their faith, yet they received their reward in heaven. Their prayers for their nation were finally being answered.

Our entrance into the occupied land of Satan was the beginning of a great triumph, yet not without trials and tribulations. We found the spirit of oppression everywhere we looked, which does not die easily. It lingered in the minds of the people and the habits of their existence. The remains of the destruction were visible in the dilapidation and greyness of everything around us, but fortunately there was an anticipation of change. The spirit of the people had to be revived to survive and thrive again as a nation after a relentless robbery. Oppression of their spirits was also evident in actions, customs, relationships, surroundings, and self-esteems. The ruins of our prospective inheritance reflected in the ruins of the spirit of the people as well. It brought me to my knees to intercede day after day for the nation and the people.

God took us out of our land to another that would be our inheritance, and little did we know the walls we would have to scale in this wilderness. It was a cold and rainy day when we first set foot on the land. I had no idea what a piece of earth would do to my life. This land we were to inherit was in central Czechoslovakia. We first arrived in Austria and traveled to Bratislava, Czechoslovakia to stay with Igor's mother, and after a few weeks we eventually took a day trip to see our inheritance first hand. It was about a three hour trip to the central part of Czechoslovakia, where Tri Duby was located. The property known as Tri Duby, translated "Three Oaks," was the place of Igor's grandfather's farmland and former place of residence. Igor had been there several years earlier, when the Russian army still occupied it. It had virtually been turned into a pig farm which fed the army, and served as a supply depot for their vodka by selling the bricks and other parts of his beautiful farm buildings on the land, which were now nothing but ruins.

On the day of our arrival, it was dreary, and there was not a very friendly welcome from the occupants on the land. Igor's mother had rented the land to pig farmers carrying on the tradition of stench, I guess. These occupiers had taken to it like it was their own, refusing to pay her a cent for almost two years, clearly breaking their written, signed contract. During Communism there was no ownership, and therefore no one understood this concept of property ownership and rental. Basically, they got away with what they could.

They did not greet us, but watched from afar, almost as though they knew something unexpected was coming. It was, but at the time, neither we nor they knew when or how. As we stood and looked across the field, as far as we could see were fields of beautiful farmland, framed with mountains in the distant horizon. It was a lovely picture that anyone would frame and put on the wall in their living room, but the beauty in our surroundings carried a deeper underlying darkness that wasn't visible to the naked eye.

Igor began to describe everything that was once there to me, where now stood only ruins. He went a short distance to a small hill to gaze out and assess the place where he had many wonderful childhood memories while my four-year-old son Michael and I waited by the car we had borrowed from my brother-in-law. I have to admit it was definitely not what I expected to see. There was a very broken down barn close by made of large stones, built in the 1800s and to my right was a herd of goats and sheep standing in front of it. I was going to snap a few pictures to take home, so I bent down to get my camera out of the case. In those days, we still used film, so while I was preparing the camera, all of a sudden, a ram charged towards my son, Michael. I saw it out of the corner of my eye, and thank God I was able to grab him and pull him out of the way, otherwise he could have ended up in the emergency room with horns dug into his head or body. Rams are known as fighting territorial animals. He must have viewed my little son, about his height, as someone to fight with for territory. Terrified and in high adrenaline mode, before I could gather my thoughts, the ram dug his heels into the ground and backed up to get speed in his next charge towards my frightened and confused son. My fight or flight adrenaline kicked in and I screamed as loud as I could to Igor for help as the ram came charging towards Michael again. Again, I screamed as loud as I could and grabbed Michael, and the ram went head first into the car, right where Michael would have been standing. By that time Igor was there and he let out a horrific scream and scared the fighting ram away. He's really good at scaring animals; I've seen it several times since. Unfortunately, the borrowed car's rear door was dented in, and we were not only very shaken, but I could think of nothing better than leaving this god-forsaken place as quickly as possible, never looking back, for fear I might turn into a pillar of salt like Lot's wife. At that very moment I declared, "This is the last time I am coming here." I could feel the evil presence still there, after this unexpected encounter.

Looking back, it is clear to me that the demonic presence lurking there definitely did not want us there. My thoughts were, "no problem, I am out of here!" But God had something else in mind. You see, there is a spiritual war going on that the naked eye cannot see, and the war is on for our very souls and destiny. All the more reason Jesus needed to come to save us, because sin has opened the door to the evil that we war against (Eph. 6:12). We need freedom from our sin, through His shed blood, to have power over the enemy in the spirit realm. No demon from hell can stand up against the power of the Holy Spirit that is given to us when we receive Christ as our Savior. I was just beginning to understand this; nothing like experience to teach me the truth.

Igor was so excited to see the property that was to be our inheritance, not because he really wanted it, but because it was a part of his past and rightfully belonged to his mother. He desired for her to have what she wanted. It was her father's land, her inheritance, stolen un-righteously, withheld for forty long years. I, on the other hand, couldn't imagine who would ever want such a horrible place.

The occupants of the property looked on from a distance, as though nothing had happened. They saw exactly what their ram did, but never even came to inquire about us or look at the car to assess the damage. I realize now they were already drowning in their guilt and who knows what else they were dealing with in those trying times making it impossible for them to face us. Guilt and shame are heavy burdens that Satan can use to keep people away from God and the abundant life He died for, as many of these people had experienced for forty years. The communist mindset was, church was just a building and God didn't live there, because according to the indoctrination of the communist regime, God did not exist.

Even though a large part of the population of the misguided people of this country believed God did not exist, He was still there. Unfortunately, their minds had been brainwashed into this very sad and broken existence. You can believe God doesn't exist, but the truth is He always was and will always be. He is the Creator of all things in the heavens and the earth, how could He not exist? The prideful man or woman that believes they are self-sufficient and in control has turned their back on God. The absence of God's presence in the lives of the atheists meant the presence of Satan in their lives. Satan wanted to rule in the Garden of Eden from the beginning, and now he was taking rulership here. When we arrived, his territory was being intruded upon and I am certain that did not settle well in the spirit world.

The Bible tells us there are spirits that rule over territories in Daniel 10:13. The prince of the kingdom of Persia was interfering with the angel that was coming to answer his prayers. There was a battle in the heavens with this prince of darkness and his demons that took more prayer and fasting to receive the victory. The angel was held up for twenty-one days, until Michael the Archangel came to his aid. The king of Persia that the angel spoke about was in the heavens, a spiritual ruler of darkness. I sensed this same kind of spiritual kingdom here in Czechoslovakia. Prayers had gone up for this nation to be free, but there was an ensuing battle going on in the heavens to overcome the powers of darkness ruling over this territory. Satan's domain was being infringed on and we could easily tell he did not like it one bit. But our God is more powerful than any demon in hell and nothing can come against Him and His children. The name of Jesus is above every name and His power is far above every other power.

> *"Therefore, God also has highly exalted Him and given Him the name which is above every name, that at the name of Jesus every knee should bow, of those in heaven, and of those on earth, and of those under the earth, and that every tongue should confess that Jesus Christ is Lord, to the glory of God the Father" (Philp. 2:9-11 NKJV).*

Spiritual Warfare

I should have known Satan was retaliating that first day when the ram charged at my son. What place to attack and hurt God's servants the most but their children. As Christians we have confidence that God is bigger than any attempt Satan can make on God's children. Even though Satan wields his power here on the earth, he cannot compare to the *Living God* and he knows it, but do we know it? I am so sure of it, yet due to circumstances and human frailties I sometimes forget, that I am who I am, by the grace of God, and that means I can do all things through Christ, who strengthens me (Phil. 4:13). These

35

small beginnings of my walk with God started to give me an inkling of knowing who I am in Christ and having real freedom from the darkness that rules in this world.

I am on the timeline God has set forth for me, just as you are, interjected with trivial and future trials. It was best I didn't know about them. There is a time for war and a time for peace (Ec. 3:8). The time for God's people to be at war in the spirit is now and always has been. Not without the understanding that He fights for us, we are the watchmen and watchwomen on the wall interceding on behalf of our own needs and the needs of people and nations. We are not alone in this battle the Lord is seated at the right hand of the Father interceding for us, who are His disciples (Heb. 7:25). I love what my friend Dale VanSteenis says about intercession. "Intercession starts in Heaven and comes to us, and then we pray. Intercession then carries our needs back to Heaven." We tend to think it is coming from us to Heaven, but it first must come down from the Holy Spirit to us in order to be able to pray.

Learning to trust in the Lord and believe His word for the promises He gave me was my first lesson in knowing the power I had in Christ. Later as I grew in the knowledge of Christ, I began to memorize scripture for every situation in my life. If I needed peace, I found what the Word of God said about peace; if I needed healing, I found the scriptures about His healing and stood on those words, wrote them down, memorized them, decreed them over my life and meditated on them day and night. The word of God became life to me, and I began to see the power of the spoken and written word of God to build my faith and change my life.

The trials we go through in life are the tools God can use

to draw us closer to Him, to gain understanding through His word of who He is and who we are in Christ. He fights for us, and no powers from hell can stand against the living God. As a teacher of the Word for many years, God never allowed me to use someone else's written Bible studies to teach. He would tell me a word to look up and take me to the concordance to study the scriptures in depth. The Bible studies were always for me first, not for others, until I learned what I was searching and studying. I spent hours and days writing and preparing for a Bible study that maybe would be only for a small group, but the fruit of it was first in me and I pray for those who heard too. Today I have His Word filed in my heart forever, and I wouldn't trade those many hours of searching and seeking Him through His word for anything.

> *"Do not be afraid nor dismayed because of this*
> *great multitude, for the battle is not yours, but*
> *God's" (2 Chron. 20:15 NKJV).*

After this unexpected battle, we packed ourselves back into the car and started our journey back to Bratislava where we were staying with family. Unfortunately, we left there with a bad taste in our mouths that for me just wouldn't go away. Satan's destructive attempts upon God's people can linger, even in the mind of a mature believer. Our minds must be renewed by the Word of God. I prayed for the Lord to plant an encouraging word in my mind, and to not let a stronghold of fear take root in my mind. Satan wants us to believe he has power, so he attempts to torment us in our minds. We can tear down every stronghold that is built in our minds with the promises in the Word of God (Phil. 2:5; 2 Cor. 10:4). I had to stand on His word for my life, my husband, and the life of my son in prayer and confession day and night, keeping my mind on Jesus and His promises. Paul said, "Let this mind be in you which was also in Christ Jesus" (Phil 2:5 NKJV). The Passion Translation says, "Let his mindset become your motivation." In other words, we have a part in or a choice to have the mind of Christ. He then describes Christ as humble bondservant who came as a man and became obedient to the point of death on the cross; exalting His name above every name and one day every tongue would confess Him as Lord to glorify God the Father (Phil. 2:6-11).

Upon returning from central Czechoslovakia, after a long journey of disappointments and trials, we had to announce to Igor's brother that his nice car had a big dent in the side from a mad ram charging it. Who would have expected that to happen to your car? We knew it would cost money to fix but unfortunately, we didn't have a dime to give him. These were just more reminders in my opinion to never go back to that God-forbidden place. In my fearful state of mind, it was like a sign went up in front of us that read "Danger, Keep Out!" An exciting adventure turned into a bad dream. I just knew I was glad to head back to my mother-in-law's apartment in Bratislava. I only knew one thing: I wanted to be as far away from Tri Duby as I could. "Linda, we can't go back there," were the words I wanted to hear Igor say. Much to my dismay, that didn't happen.

-8-

OUT OF MY COMFORT ZONE

I loved the adventure of a new place, yet something was just not quite right. Even Igor's mother seemed to be sometimes leery of us "Americans." At times she seemed almost angry at us, because we were Americans. Although I understood the communists, for all those years, had brainwashed the people to believe that Americans were "Capitalist Pigs" and were their biggest enemy during the cold war. I determined perhaps that was the problem when I tried to understand some of the behaviors of a culture that was totally new to me. After I experienced relationships with the people, I grew to love them with the love of Jesus and know them as a meek and humble people.

So much was different to me, especially the trust and compassion for others I always had, but it seemed missing here. My best description is the Communist oppression stole their joy and peace; it also stole their trust and compassion for others. Later we found out that it was a common way of making money by snitching on your neighbor, so you really never knew when you were being spied on. Even in our rides on the tram with Igor's mother, she would tell us to be quiet when we talked about the property for fear someone would hear.

What a shame to have to live under fear, hiding and being secretive about everything.

When many people think of love, they think of a romantic novel or movie, full of gush and kisses and romantic bliss, but no one really knows the true love that only Christ can give until they encounter Him personally in relationship. In an environment where God is absent for so long it was hard to imagine how the fruit of love could be evident. Although, not all was bad; it was through relationship we grew to love our Slovak friends and family.

We were treated with a great deal of hospitality and kindness by family and friends in an attempt to make our stay good. Unfortunately, for so many Slovaks, something very important was missing from their lives and their culture—God Himself. All that I grew up with did not fit into this strange land. I wondered how could I as an American ever find my place here? A question only time could answer.

Looking back on this time of my life it is clear to me that God knew and allowed Communism to fall exactly when He did, so that we and so many others could go to this once captive nation to set the captives free with Jesus. I did not yet realize that we fit into a larger picture that expanded to the realms of the universe and it was all in God's perfect timing.

I reflect now on all the sacrifices made by all those who went before us, who suffered, died, and were tortured for their faith. I count it a blessing to suffer for Christ and am thankful that I have not gone through what the saints who lived and died for their faith during the Communist regime did.

*"And they overcame him by the blood of the Lamb
and by the word of their testimony, and they did not
love their lives to the death" (Rev. 12:11 NKJV).*

Time to Leave

Our one-month stay was coming to a close, after meeting Igor's wonderful family and countless friends. We had sampled a variety of very tasty Slovak dishes and took sightseeing tours to see some beautiful castles and historic sights. While I was centered on myself, which is the demon of all demons in this life, I was relieved to once again be heading back to my comfort zone, America. One nation under God, the land that I love, which was magnified even more after this trip!

Michael, who was a typical kid, loved our visit and all the new adventures he experienced. He made friends so easily and was overjoyed to have two new cousins and two new grandparents, who quickly grew to love him. I was so welcomed by everyone, not to mention it was my first time in Europe (a lifelong dream), although might I say Paris or Rome could have been much more romantic and enjoyable! Needless to say, this is where God wanted me to be; what was He thinking? Or better yet, what was I not seeing in this picture?

Igor went through many adjustments in the process of his time there after so many years of absence. After his miraculous escape in 1966, he had only been home once. Reintegrating into one's family after years of absence is not always smooth. Jesus himself was not appreciated by His home town of Nazareth. The people saw Him as just the son of Joseph the carpenter and consequently, after hearing Him read the scripture in the synagogue, those who heard Him speak were filled with wrath at Him, implying that he was fulfilling these words of the prophet Isaiah. "The Spirit of the Lord is upon me, because he hath anointed me to preach the gospel to the poor; he hath sent me to heal the brokenhearted, to preach deliverance to the captives, and recovering of sight to the blind, to set at liberty them that are bruised, [19]To preach the acceptable year of the Lord" (Luke 4:18, 19 KJV).

After He sat down, He continued to answer their questions and give them more wisdom and they became enraged at Him. What they did next was amazing: they "rose up and thrust Him out of the city; and they led Him to the brow of the hill on which their city was built, that they might throw Him down over the cliff. Then passing through the midst of them, He went his way" (Luke 4:29, 30 NKJV). He escaped supernaturally, because He was not only the man Jesus, but God. He went on to Capernaum and did great things. Sometimes we must leave our hometown and go where God sends us to fulfill His plan for our lives.

Igor was a full-fledged American and prouder than just about anyone I know of being a citizen. Immigrants are truly thankful for their freedoms, especially when they come from countries that were under tyranny and their lives were in danger. During our stay he made sure everyone knew how proud he was to be an American. Even I was a little taken back by his American pride. I love my country dearly, but unlike him I couldn't quite get as excited about it as he did, because I had not yet learned to appreciate it. God was preparing me on this trip for what He had in store for my life in the years to come, and through experience I would learn to appreciate where He birthed me more and more. The furthest thing from my mind was living anywhere else except the good old USA, especially after this trip.

God is full of surprises; I have learned that the thing that we think we will do with our life is not always what God has for us. Some people know exactly what they are called to be even from a young age. I know people who said as a child they would be a doctor or a teacher or an artist and it goes that way, but I never knew what I would be. As I drew closer to Jesus, I began to pray a simple prayer daily, "Here I am Lord, use me." and that gave Him permission to do what I could not imagine or ever hope to accomplish or become. Try it. You might be surprised what God does in your life.

At this point in my life, I only wanted to settle back into my comfortable life as I knew it, raise my son, and be "happy." What being happy was to me was not what God had in mind. God knows how much we can endure and prepares us to be able to endure through it all. He knows our future and reveals it to us, in what seems like puzzle pieces, so we don't run and hide in a cave in the mountains and never come out again or run ahead of Him and make a major disaster trying to do what we think is His will. Jeremiah stated it so well, "For I know the thoughts that I think toward you, says the LORD, thoughts of peace and not of evil, to give you a future and a hope" (Jer. 29:11 NKJV).

-9-

BACK HOME IN OUR COMFORT ZONE

Igor and I were not your usual people living in an apartment or house. As I told you before, we lived in upstate New York in a huge, abandoned factory building on the top floor, with 6,000 sq. ft. of open air space and fifty-two windows…perfect for two artists. It is said that artists think different and are sometimes capable of doing things a lot different than the run of the mill. By all standards we fit the description; by our life-style, our adventurous nature, and risk taking, which is hard to understand by many people's standards. It was a fun and adventurous life for us all. If Michael wanted to, he was able to ride his bicycle, roller skate, and play soccer and basketball in our loft with the neighborhood kids. He was such a giving person from a very young age; it was not uncommon for him to give his toys away. I would look out the window of the loft and see one of the boys taking his basketball home, after they had played. Even in the park, as a two-year-old, he would share his toys in the sandbox. This was an amazing little boy God gave us.

Igor had lived in this loft for seventeen years before I met him, and now he shared his grungy cluttered bachelor space with a meticulous woman and a bouncy little boy. Of course, when a woman moves in it means change, especially the arrangements for living. A man can survive with just about any arrangement, but a woman needs to build her nest. There wasn't a place to really prepare a meal, so we built a kitchen area. It was very cold in the winter, sometimes down to -23 degrees, so I had to wear gloves with the fingertips cut out to cook, and we wore long underwear and layers of clothes all day long, but it never crossed my mind that was unusual. In fact, we were never sick; germs can't live in a cold place, so I count it as another blessing from the Lord. Many other things needed to be added to our home, so we added a door on the bathroom (imagine no door on the bathroom), and a place to sleep with heat (not asking too much right?). We did this by building walls of plastic with an added propane heater and had electric blankets too. We made a large room with a wood burning stove and a huge, heavy door that closed off the room for our living room. Well, before you knew it, we were working day and night building a house within our factory. Joyfully, it was starting to feel and look like a home.

Igor was a great handyman, so he was always busy doing something to make me happy and I would help, with his direction, which sometimes was a little too over-directing for my style. We were in the midst of getting to know each other, along with unloading all the baggage we both brought into our relationship from our past. It was a real dumping ground for several years. My suitcase was always packed just in case I had to get out quickly, which I occasionally did for a few hours. Little did I know I was running from my selfish pride, which is another evil that must die in every Christian. To God be all the glory that we didn't kill each other or go completely crazy in the midst of the baggage dumping. The Lord was never so gracious as He was to us those first years. Our one saving grace was that we were both committed to seeking the Lord with all our hearts and all our souls, and teaching Michael to do the same, even though we were far from accomplishing a perfect Christian life. "For all have sinned and fall short of the glory of God" (Rom. 3:23 NKJV). A big AMEN to that!

I thank God for the Holy Spirit and the conviction of our sin, so that we could repent and change with His help and His grace that covers us, when we don't deserve it and definitely can't do it ourselves.

Life as Usual

From our adventure in post-communism land, we arrived back to our wonderful life and had our ten rolls of film processed and proceeded to digest our journey to Czechoslovakia into the past. At least that's what we thought. When God calls you to a place, it just doesn't disappear, it keeps coming after you. We shared all our adventurous experiences and the distress we felt about the ruins of the nation and the lives we saw by the intruder named Communism. There was so much to tell and remember; we went on for months sharing it with our friends, and talking between us about what we experienced, along with still trying to understand it all. Our lives went on as usual. I went back to my job working in a shelter for homeless teenagers, where I was learning a lot. Even though I had just come out of a complete breakdown, from a lot of poor choices, and difficult results from those choices, there is no better way to find peace again than to help others. Helping these lost, confused teenagers was a blessing and a challenge at the same time, but also a training ground for future things God called me too. There is not one thing we go through that does not lead to something else God has written in our book in heaven. Sometimes it is a step in the right direction and sometimes a wrong step that must be righted by the hand of God moving in our lives. I am thankful that the Lord God Almighty has His hand on me guiding my life into the place He designed. Paul suffered a thorn in his side that he pleaded with God to remove, but God's answer to him was, "My grace is sufficient for you, for my strength is made perfect in weakness" (2 Cor. 12:9 NKJV).

In the midst of his trials, Paul learned to rejoice and boast in his infirmities that the power of Christ would rest on him. It's not living in a comfort zone, but a life of challenges in trials, with tempering and transforming, that make us more like Jesus. If we want to be fruit producers, this is what it takes.

-IO-

HEARING THE CALL

Life went on at its usual pace. We got up each day, read the Bible and prayed together to start our day and ended it in the same way. The Lord started to work in us both, to clean out the garbage we both carried from our past. It felt like fire from Heaven was coming down on us and was about to destroy us. I think of the story in the book of Daniel where the King commanded that everyone bow down and worship the golden image that the king had set up. Shadrach, Meshach, and Abednego refused, and the king ordered the fire in the furnace be heated up seven times hotter before he threw them into it. They had faith that their God would save them, and He did. Even the king was convinced that he was the son of God (Daniel 3:10,17, 25 NKJV). It felt like we had been thrown into the fire and we definitely needed a Savior.

Some people think that God doesn't speak to us, but I guess they haven't read the Bible. He spoke to people throughout the Old and New Testament. I also believe that God has never changed, as His word says, "Jesus Christ is the same yesterday, today, and forever" (Heb. 13:8 NKJV). There are so many great examples in the Bible of God speaking to His people. Moses was one that God spoke to face to face as a man speaks to a friend (Ex. 33:11a). I would not have been saved if I hadn't heard the voice of Jesus speaking to me in that church in Monroe, New York. God can speak to us any way He chooses. Jesus left us the Holy Spirit to guide us, as our Helper, to remind us of all the things Jesus said and to give us revelation of them. He will speak to us through His Word, in dreams and visions, through prophets and words of knowledge or wisdom from men and women of God and sometimes through angels. We hear God's voice in many different ways.

God didn't leave us alone; He said He never leaves us or forsakes us (Heb. 13:5). The Holy Spirit's still small voice can speak to us, as it did to the prophet Elijah. The Lord was not in the wind, not in the earthquake, and not in the fire, but then he heard a still small voice (1 Kings 19:11, 12).

Since my conversion to Christianity a few years earlier, I experienced the awesome presence of God when I read the Bible and prayed, but I had not heard God speak to me since my first encounter with Him in the church in Monroe, although I was about to. I just love the way God sneaks up on you and surprises you with things you would have never dreamed of happening. I heard one preacher call Him "Jehovah Sneaky," so funny but true. I do think God has a sense of humor too.

God was about to give me the first inkling that change was coming. It happened one day as I was outside on the back stairs of our loft hanging up the laundry next to a very big mulberry tree. The bows of this big tree draped in front of where I was hanging out the wet clothes to dry on our manmade pulley clothesline. Imagine, I was in the act of laundry duty and I heard the still small voice of the Holy Spirit utter these words in my head, "When you see the fruit ripe on this tree, you will be gone from here." I thought to myself what…gone from where, this factory, this city, just what did that mean? I pretended like I didn't hear these words at first, but they kept playing like a broken record in my mind and every time I went outside by that tree I kept looking at the fruit, watching to see if it was ripe yet. When I first heard these words, the fruit was still white and green, so there were several months to go until it turned a deep purple, ready to pick and eat. Over the next few weeks that still small voice kept speaking to me with persistence. One day while putting the dishes away in our open-air kitchen, I heard another message from that same still small voice of the Holy Spirit. His sweet quite voice said, "You will live in Slovakia, and I will give you all you need…don't worry about what you will eat or where you will live." I certainly didn't want to hear that. Despite my dislike of that thought, I started to imagine how this could possibly be, remembering our visit with some fear and dismay. Even though I tried to forget these words, God was speaking to me through His Word, daily confirming these words uttering over and over in my head. I knew they were not my thoughts or words, but His. He was preparing me for something much bigger than I could ever even imagine at this time.

Usually, people get confused about what the difference is between their thoughts—thoughts planted by demon spirits, and God's thoughts. One easy way to know is, if it lines up with the Word of God, then it is from God. Is it something you would have thought of normally? Then it is yours. Is it something totally out of your character or downright evil or sinful?

Then it is from the devil. God always confirms His words.

Now the words I heard were an instruction that I never would have thought of. It wasn't evil or going to cause me to sin, so it couldn't have been the Enemy. It was persistent and being affirmed in God's word, so I began to understand it was from God. One scripture He gave me to confirm His word was to Abraham: "By faith Abraham obeyed when he was called to go out to the place which he would receive as an inheritance. And he went out, not knowing where he was going" (Hebrews 11:8 NKJV).

All God wanted was my obedience like Abraham, who was called to leave his country and go where God was sending him. The Bible says without faith it is impossible to please God; we must believe He is who He is and that He rewards those who diligently seek Him (Heb. 11:6). We walk by faith not sight (2 Cor. 5:7); faith is just trusting God, even when we can't understand or see what He is asking us to do. God was requiring something of me that I could not see, believe, or even imagine at this point, but He would not leave me without all that I needed. He reassured me through His word and His promises to me. He promised in His Word that we did not need to fear or be dismayed, but only to trust in Him to take care of all our needs, as He spoke to Joshua, "Have I not commanded you? Be strong and of good courage; do not be afraid, nor be dismayed, for the LORD your God is with you wherever you go" (Joshua 1:9 NKJV).

One of my favorite characters in the Bible is Joshua. Here was a young man who was being prepared by God to take over the place of Moses and enter into the Promised Land in his place. What a daunting task that must have been for a young man, to follow in Moses' footsteps. God spoke to him and encouraged him to take the steps necessary to complete this task, to trust Him, and to not fear. Joshua knew the Law or the Torah, which was filed in his heart and mind. God wanted him to know that he could do anything if he just believed His Word, meditated on it day and night, and did what it instructed him to do. If he would do what God asked of him, then his way would be made straight and he would prosper and have success in what God called him to do (Joshua 1:8). This was my lesson, even though I was not going to the Promise Land for Israel, it was the promise land for the ministry that God called me to. God said to Joshua, "No man shall be able to stand before you all the days of your life; as I was with Moses, so I will be with you. I will not leave you or forsake you" (Joshua 1:5 NKJV).

I was learning that God had a plan for my life that I could not understand at that time, but all I had to do was trust Him and go where He was sending me. I was also reminded of the prayer that I said faithfully, "Here I am Lord, use me." Did I not expect God to answer my prayer? He always listens and answers. I needed to just believe Him and His Word and accept the call on my life to glorify Him in every way.

What about you? What is God asking you to do? For those who are obedient love Him.

-II-

ENCOUNTERING THE VOICE
OF THE HOLY SPIRIT

Knowing the voice of the Holy Spirit is clearly something all true believers need to have assurance about. Many times, people say "something told me or I just had this feeling," but often that something or feeling is the third person of God, the Holy Spirit. He wants to speak to us and guide us through the trials and circumstances of our life that are troubling or to bring conviction of our sin and change us by leading us to the truth (John 16:8, 13). The Holy Spirit was sent from God to be our helper and comforter; a consuming fire to bring conviction of sin; as a rushing mighty wind, and looking like tongues of fire to baptize and empower (Acts 2:2). Appearing as a dove when Jesus was baptized by John (Matt. 3:16); He is the Spirit of Truth, guiding us into the truth (John 16:13). Every believer is called to hear from God through His Word, however, God also chooses to speak to us, as I said earlier, however we will listen, whether in a dream, through a song or a book, through a prophet, a teacher, a brother or sister in Christ, or through His still small voice (1 Kings 19:12). When God's word comes, it is important that it falls on good soil, so it can take root and bear fruit. God speaks, but do we listen and do we take it to heart and trust Him to fulfill what He said? It was up to me to have a willing heart, to trust Him to do what He said, and to step out in obedience, so that fruit could be produced.

As I stated earlier, when I first met Jesus, I was stunned to hear a still small voice speaking to me after I simply said, "Please Jesus, help me," while I knelt alone in a church in my broken, desperate condition in life. I heard in my left ear, "You have gone astray, but now you have come back. I have never left you, now take my hand and I will take you through everything." These were life changing words for me, even though I didn't understand exactly what they meant at the time. When I heard those words, God began to do something in my life that I could have never imagined, and it is still happening for thirty-two years now. He was holding my hand and guiding me through the shadow of the valley of death of my selfish life without hope. Jesus came to transform me and change me; He never wanted me to sit in my selfishness looking for my next blessing from Him. He wanted me to step out in total faith that He could do the impossible in my life, that clearly had very little hope. The only way for that to happen was to walk by faith and not by sight. The Holy Spirit was guiding me, and leading me to the truth. I knew Jesus in my head and through His Word, but I needed a deep encounter with Him, and that meant intimacy and wonder with Him, to meet Him face to face.

Jesus said, "My sheep know my voice, and I know them, and they follow Me." (John 10:27 NKJV). His voice is the voice of God, and we can hear Him, when we commune with Him daily in prayer, meditate on His Word, worship and praise Him. If we draw near to Him, He will draw near to us. His wonder doesn't come by sitting in a comfortable place never taking risks, never stepping out in faith, never being tried and tested by distresses, pains, and struggles; it is a wilderness journey that we must enter into to become that vessel of honor for His glory. My wilderness journey had begun in Monroe, New York, destitute of comfort in a familiar place, destitute of family support, destitute of any material means to do anything, destitute of anything aside from the love of God and His Holy Spirit to guide me into the desert places, for my training in experiencing God in His fullness and wonder. I am so grateful for those wilderness days looking back. I can't imagine where I would be without them!

God's Word Being Planted

A few weeks had passed since I stood outside by that mulberry tree and heard the still small voice of the Holy Spirit speaking to me. Yet His words were still in my heart and mind and now I was about to find out just how they would come to pass. As things go in life, one day Igor unexpectedly looked out the window from the top floor of the loft and there was a man in his business clothes looking at the first floor of the building with a clipboard in his hand and writing with a pen in the other. Igor yelled out the window to him and asked what he was doing. He said he was an inspector for the city. For some unknown reason Igor invited him in to see where we lived, unbeknownst to him that we could legally be thrown out. And you guessed it; he sent a notice to the building owner that we could not legally live there, after Igor had lived there for seventeen years.

After four years of going through the wilderness and consuming fire previous to this, it was a continuation of stripping away the layers of immediate comfort and familiar territory since my conversion as a Jesus follower. We managed to stay another two months thanks to the law being on our side, just enough time for the mulberries to ripen. God fulfills His word and He always does it His way!

We commenced to hanging a sheet from the windows on the top floor of the building for two months, with large letters saying, "MOVING SALE." After having sold almost all of our worldly belongings, we moved to a friend's to decide where we would go next. Unbelievably, our final conclusion was Czechoslovakia, just as the Lord had spoken to me. Why is it so hard to accept change and trust that God's way is always the best way? There is a path set for us, and if we trust in Him, we will find that path. We just have to believe His word (Prov. 3:5, 6).

Moving is one of the most difficult things to do, which I had already been through numerous times in the previous years. This time it brought me to the end of all material belongings except clothes and bare essentials. I had to let go of everything, which was a real test of my faith. I had already rid myself of many worldly belongings, but I hung onto what I thought I still needed, or should I say, all those things I held absolutely impossible to part with. Possessions can possess us, if we are not careful. You know those important things like a TV, tapes (no CDs in those days), books, dishes, and the many paintings I did over the years. They had to go too. You've heard that saying, your junk is another man's treasure. We even sold a rock for three dollars! It must have had some kind of power attached to it, like I thought in my New Age days. Even after two months of selling things at the loft, I still had to have garage sales to cleanse the final things from my life; I couldn't take them with me, could I?

We sold everything, bought a van, our airline tickets, and shipped the van on an ocean liner to Germany, where we could retrieve it in six weeks. It was not possible to imagine what God had in store for us, in our next journey to Czechoslovakia, but it did come just as God said it would. The fruit was ripe on the mulberry tree and we had vacated our loft and were headed to another nation. I had to trust that God would provide everything we needed, because He said He would. My confirmation was in His word, "Therefore do not worry, saying, 'What shall we eat?' or 'What shall we drink?' or 'What shall we wear?' For after all these things the Gentiles seek. For your heavenly Father knows that you need all these things. But seek first the kingdom of God and His righteousness, and all these things shall be added to you" (Matt. 6:31-33 NKJV). Later, this scripture was on my refrigerator to remind me daily of this truth, as I was walking it out in life.

The confirmation to move to Slovakia (which was the former Czechoslovakia, now divided into two nations, the Slovak Republic and the Czech Republic) came in several letters from Igor's mom over that past year, saying she wanted to give us Tri Duby, and she would help us to develop it if we would come. She made many promises and after several letters and phone conversations, Igor started to think it would be a good option. I resisted the idea; it was not my idea of what I wanted to do with the rest of my life. Who needed that piece of land anyway, where goats ram into your car and thieves live. I could not bear the thought of being so far away from all my family, even though they were already estranged from me during those years; even though I lived with hope for a change and my dear country and comfortable familiar life. To tell the truth, I was scared to death to take such a drastic step. Thanks to Igor and his strong faith, I was able to go in faith, with his arm holding me up and dragging me to the plane. I had to remind myself over and over, when I am weak the Lord is strong (2 Cor. 12:10). I never needed God's supernatural strength as much as I did then. I had to obey what He had spoken to me, if I wanted to see fruit in my life and I certainly didn't want to end up like Jonah, in the belly of a whale!

-12-

ON TO BE A NEW CREATION/
THE SEND

When someone receives Jesus Christ as their Savior, scripture tells us we are a "new creation; old things have passed away; behold all things have become new" (2 Cor. 5:17 NKJV). So far, I did not understand what that meant, but God was determined that I did become that new creation and put away all the old. I had to continue on in my wilderness experience to find who I was called to be and first of all, who Jesus was to me. The Israelites crossed over the Red Sea on dry ground, they left everything behind, except the bare necessities and the treasures of gold and jewels that God gave them before leaving. God opened the way for them to go to a comfortable life—not! He opened the way for them to enter into the wilderness to find who He was and then know who they were with Him. Forty years of wandering, complaining, and failing to get the message, but God persisted with them by His amazing mercy and grace, generation after generation, to move those who remained to the Promised Land.

Little did I know I was headed to the wilderness to be tempered and tried, until I knew who God was and knew who I was in Christ, to be transformed by His amazing grace and love and become a new creation. I told you Igor and I both brought a lot of past garbage into our lives together. I realized I hadn't seen anything yet. One way to get that garbage out was to put pressure on to force it out. Whoever invented the trash compacter had a great idea, because garbage can take over and become stinky and too much to get rid of after some time. It's like that with us humans, our garbage can build up and get pretty stinky in our lives and we don't know where to put it or how to get rid of it or hide it any longer.

My trash compacter was working with the trials of being an immigrant, unable to speak the language, not having access to a television, and there were no cell phones then. I couldn't call a friend or family to help me; my prayer partner was in New York and I could only write letters, which took weeks to send or receive. I was definitely out of my comfort zone. My pain was deep, my disappointments were many, and my past failed relationships left deep wounds in my heart and my mind. My view of myself was less than good. All I knew was that I loved Jesus and I wanted to do His will with my life. Here I was, and here I had to stay whether I liked it or not, because I had no place else to run.

I thank God Igor's family took us in and gave us love and acceptance. I had to adapt to the ways of shopping and going to the post office in our little area of town in order to be able to do anything on my own. I learned to ride the trams and found a church I liked, even though I couldn't understand a word they were saying; thank God for some translators at times. The good news was that I had a lot of time to listen and not speak, it was my training in listening to the Holy Spirit, and amazingly He helped me to understand what was going on, even when I didn't understand the language. After a few months, I was beginning to feel a little bit at home regardless of the very complicated situation I found myself. Thank God for Igor and his patience with me and his constant translation for me to understand anything at all. I have deep compassion for immigrants. I come from a long line of them, first born in my family in America was my dad and mom. My great-grandparents and grandparents on both sides were born in Germany and the Ukraine and immigrated to America in the late 1800s and early 1900s. One of my grandmothers never learned to write very well in English and spoke several different languages when she spoke, sometimes, German, Russian, and English mixed. Fortunately, I had developed an ear for listening to foreign languages because I grew up around German speaking people and it was somewhat familiar to me. I can only imagine what they went through coming to America. Igor was also an immigrant, so he understood what that was like also. They were trying days of adjustment for me, but by God's grace and strength I made it through.

As I said earlier, when we are struggling, the best way to overcome is to help someone else that is struggling. God planted people in our path continuously to help and to care for; everyone from gypsies to hitchhikers, to the regular people we met in family situations or church. We acted like the good Samaritans, when it came to giving of ourselves and what we had to others. Isn't that what being a Christian is all about? We soon realized this was not the way of those around us. Gypsies were known to be liars and thieves; according to the good advice of others we were to stay clear of them, even according to some Christians. But we did what we knew God wanted us to do and not to please man. Letting go of my life of self-consumption and over-strategizing what I should do or how I felt, slowly I became more in touch with who God called me to be, a servant and His friend. I needed Jesus more than I could ever imagine. After panic attacks, fears, heart-breaks, and disappointments in myself and others, needless to say, I was a basket case half of the time. But somewhere in the midst of all the chaos I began to love the people around me and the simplicity of my new life, and I began to feel peace now and then especially when I drew near to God. The closer I drew to God the closer He drew to me and the more peace and faith I had (James 4:8). It's amazing how that works, I can't explain it, but it works that way. If you are living in fear or in deep trouble, draw near to God. He will step in and do what you are not able to do. It is a promise to His children.

Paralyzing Fear vs. Love

> *"For God has not given us a spirit of fear, but of power and of love and of a sound mind"*
> *(2 Tim. 1:7 NKJV).*

There were a lot of old ways and thinking to be healed in me. I had panic attacks from age thirteen to fifty. It was during this time of stress and uncertainty in my life that I began to have them more and more frequently. I even developed a fear of having an attack, which would of course lead to an attack. If you have never had a panic attack, it is a terrifying feeling that makes you believe you will die, your heart pounds so fast you cannot breath, and you feel one breath away from death. In my case, I heard over and over in my mind, "you are going to die," which escalated everything even more.

These attacks began some years after my grandfather died, who I was very close to. When I went into a hospital, a church, or a funeral during my teen and young adult life, I would have a panic attack. Little did I realize they stemmed back to my memories of his death. I was in the hospital the night of his passing from cancer, plus all the memories of going through the three-day German Catholic wake kneeling next to his body saying the rosary. As grandchildren, we were asked to kneel before his body to say the rosary; it was agonizing to be so close to his dead lifeless body for me as a child. I didn't understand the whole thing of death. I saw my mom cry for the first time, I saw his body lying there not breathing, lifeless. I knew I could never talk to him or sit on his lap again, or hang out with him in his shop, which I did often as a child. I was devastated, but didn't know how to express how I felt to anyone, and the sad part was no one asked.

Instead, my internalized fear of death showed up in my life during panic attacks and came with a vengeance, at traumatic times in my life such as when I went through a divorce and lost custody of my step-son along with my husband, or when a friend died, or I had to go to the hospital to visit someone or to the doctor when I was sick or injured. They came relentlessly, especially under stress or when I was abandoned and alone. It was the abandonment and loss that was a real trigger in my case.

Every person has a root cause of their fears. I didn't discover the root cause of my panic attacks until I was fifty years old, but God revealed to me I had a fear of death. I realized that God had given me a promise of eternal life and the fear of death was a lie that the enemy had used to build a stronghold in my mind, during the death of my grandfather. When we accept a lie in our minds, the enemy will use it to begin building a stronghold that will hold us in a pattern of fear, failure, self-hatred, addictions, or a multitude of false beliefs to paralyze us and stop the plan God has for our lives. Satan's ultimate goal is to stop our destiny and destroy us.

The Apostle Paul instructs us to take charge of our thoughts by, "casting down arguments and every high thing that exalts itself against the knowledge of God, bringing every thought into captivity to the obedience of Christ" (2 Cor. 10:5 NKJV).

I had to learn that the love of God had set me free of all fear, because His word has given me assurance of who I am in Christ. We must have our minds transformed by the Word of God, which is the truth. So, every time I heard the words in my head "you are going to die" in the middle of a panic attack, I began to speak the truth, from the Word of God back to myself and to the Enemy attacking my mind. I took every thought captive in obedience to Christ. Over time, when I felt a panic attack coming on, I could stop it with the truth of the Word of God, by speaking it out loud to myself and the panic attack would last for only a moment or not even happen. I was renewing my mind with the Word of God.

My power was in Jesus' name and His Word, but I had to know who I was in Christ and learn to use this weapon of great power to overcome the attempt of the enemy to destroy me, to paralyze me and steal my peace and joy of the Lord, which is my strength. We are endued with power from the Holy Spirit, full of love. When Jesus lives in us, we are given a sound mind. We have received the mind of Christ, which gives us all we need for this life.

-13-

GET PERSONAL WITH YOUR SAVIOR

Developing a relationship with Jesus Christ our Savior is transforming, renewing, and revealing. Transforming, because He transforms us by cleansing us from our past, step by step, slowly making us into the "new creations" we are to be, in Him. Intimacy with the Lord is renewing, by the power of His Word that wipes out all the lies of the enemy in our minds and renews our thinking and our understanding of who we are. Revealing, when He begins to uncover things in the dark corners of our heart and mind that separate us from Him and others, hence drawing us closer to Him, and we begin to look more and more like Him.

His love is manifest in us through the changes that take place as our relationship with Him grows deeper and deeper still. In the worst of times, God can seem so far away that we have to do everything in our power to remember He is not far from us. It may not be clear by how we feel or by our circumstances. We must remember, it is a faith walk, not by sight or our feelings, but by our trust in Him no matter how little it might be. At this time of my life, my faith was small like a mustard seed, but I knew my God was big, and He always brought me through no matter how big the mountain was.

During these trials, I learned to pray in a new way, with power and travail, persevering with His amazing grace. I held on to His promises: "I say to you, if you have faith as a mustard seed, you will say to this mountain, 'Move from here to there,' and it will move; and nothing will be impossible for you" (Matt. 17:20 NKJV).

His promises are food for our starving souls, the answers to our many problems, and with a little bit of faith we can move those mountains out of the way. I was able to move this mountain of fear and panic out of my life, through the tools of my redemption in Christ. His name, above every name, His Word, the truth against every lie of the enemy, His blood, which cleansed me of all my sins, and the praise and worship I felt in my heart for Him.

Overcoming through Intimacy

The Psalmist wrote in Psalms 42:1 NKJV, "As the deer pants after water brooks, so my soul pants after You, O God." He is in deep anguish and cannot even eat, longing for the presence of God, even as those around him are mocking Him. Verse 4 continues, "My tears have been my food day and night, while they continually say to me, "Where is my God?" I love what The Passion Translation says, "Where is this God of yours? Why doesn't he help you?" Just like the Enemy, to mock God and try to get us to give up. But the psalmist encouraged himself by remembering when he went into the house of God, "with the voice of joy and praise, with a multitude that kept a pilgrim feast (the Holy Days)." He found joy and peace in going amongst other believers to worship God. In a strange new land, I found a church and connected with people with like minds and a love for the living God, Jesus Christ, this changed everything for me. In the midst of my trials and difficulties I was also drawing nearer to God and He was in turn drawing near to me. I knew God was near to me in my intimate time with Him because I heard His voice and His Word became living and powerful to me teaching me the way to go. He was the only source of comfort and hope I could run too.

The Psalmist talks to himself in verse 5: "Why are you cast down, O my soul? And why are you disquieted within me? Hope in God, for I shall yet praise Him for the help of His countenance." When we look to Jesus and recognize who He is and what He has done for us, as we go deeper into His word, we begin to understand even with our humanistic approach to God, how much He loves us. Life takes on a new view, as we turn a corner and draw closer to our Savior in an intimate relationship through prayer, worship and meditation on His Word. We begin to see life differently and most of all, ourselves and others differently.

When our relationship with Jesus becomes more intimate, our obsession with self becomes less and less dominant. Jesus taught those who are first will be last and those who are last will be first in the kingdom of God (Matt. 19:30; 20:16). The rewards of the believer will not be given according to the world's standards, but Heaven's standards, which are not what we think we deserve.

The Psalmist begins to see who God is in the midst of his pain and troubled heart and begins to pray by crying out to God his deepest feelings. Verse 6 says, "O my God, my soul is cast down within me; Therefore I will remember You from the land of Jordan, And from the heights of Hermon, From the Hill Mizar. Deep calls unto deep at the noise of Your waterfalls. All your waves and billows have gone over me. The Lord will command His lovingkindness in the daytime, and in the night His song shall be with me—A prayer to the God of my life."

This is his prayer, a prayer of his complaints to God and talking to himself instead of God, as though he is just reminding himself that God's got this, if only he can remember who God is and that He is his only hope. Sometimes it is all we can do to just remind ourselves that God's got this. If He truly is God and we believe He is who He says He is, then we have to trust Him and believe He will do what He says. His Word tells us His promises and we must simply decree them and believe them. Rather than focus on what the devil or demons are doing, it is more constructive to look at all that God has done and will do. "Enter His gates with thanksgiving and into His courts with praise" (Ps. 100:4 NKJV). When we begin to thank the Lord, we can enter into His presence. In His presence is where miracles can happen. Impossible things can be moved out of the way miraculously.

You might be saying you have tried that but things just got worse. Well, join the club of believers that have been through many trials and tests and things got worse, before they got better. Ask yourself, did you still praise God, did you draw closer to Him, did you stand on His promises, did you rejoice always, did you count all your blessings and give thanks in everything and most of all did you get through it all in God's time and way?

Being a mature Christian is what we all hope to achieve and going through the hard things is what gets us to that place of deep calling to deep as much as we don't like it. My hope is in Him, not myself. My mantra is "Less of me and more of you, Jesus." That is a fearful thing to say, because it means striping away of all that is comfortable and in your control in order to transition into knowing Him, not just in word, but truly knowing and understanding who He is. The glorious result of this is that we are then prepared to make Him known to all we meet. When you have a revelation of this truth, you have found your purpose.

-14-

GOD KNOWS THE HOUR

The Bible says that no one except the Father knows the hour of Jesus' return (Matt. 24:36). God's timing is amazing; He is in control, and yet we have to give him our control to let Him work. We do have a part to play in the big picture. We need to see our own lives in the bigger picture not just in the present me-isms. When I realized that this life was not mine but the Lord's, I began to understand that it was a set-up by God. Communism fell in 1989; my son, Michael was born in 1989; I ended up in New York, destitute without hope and met Jesus in 1991; and then I met Igor, who was about to be called to Czechoslovakia to help his mom. Could I have planned all that? I don't think so. I believe God had it planned all along. Even when we go the wrong way, He has His ways of bringing us back on track. The many left and right turns I took off the path would, by His grace, prove to be the groundwork for soul winning and testimony giving that changed lives, not just mine.

A huge task was set before us in a strange land that I did not fully understand. Have you ever felt like a fish out of water? I completely understand the plights of an immigrant in a strange land. We have our own ways of thinking and doing things from our upbringing and culture, but when we find ourselves in a new culture, it takes time to adapt and find our way. Abraham was called out of his homeland of Ur into a strange and unknown land (Gen. 12:1). He obeyed God and went to a place unknown to him, to do things for a people he did not know. God counted his obedience in faith as righteousness and gave him rewards he could never imagine.

And he believed in the LORD, and He accounted it to him for righteousness. Then He said to him, "I am the LORD, who brought you out of Ur of the Chaldeans, to give you this land to inherit it" (Gen. 15:6, 7 NKJV).

Forty Years of Communism

Occupation of the family farmland by the Russian army took place in 1950. As a small boy, Igor witnessed the communist officials coming to his childhood "happy place" and turning their lives upside down. What was once a thriving beautiful farm his grandfather and many others had worked and prospered from for many years, was now by admission of the government the worst pollution spot in the whole country. This was verified to us as we saw a documentary about Tri Duby (the location of the farm land, translated "Three Oaks"), our future inheritance, being ranked as the most polluted place in the country. That fateful day of occupation the communist officials carried a small box containing beetles and planted them in the storage bin of grain and then accused his grandfather of destroying the grain with pests. They ordered him to take everything out of his pockets and turn over all his belongings to them, even down to a pitchfork. Even though that day was dreadful and fearful, Igor's mother had a list of every piece of property they took. Later this would prove to be of great value to us because we received the right to retrieve everything stolen in restitution, so they had to give us the value of everything in return.

Igor's grandfather was sentenced to seven years in prison for being a bourgeoisie. After one year, he was released because of favors performed to the high communist officials by Igor's father, who was the first plastic surgeon and founder of plastic surgery in Czechoslovakia. After his release from prison, his grandfather came back to the communist occupied farm to labor and toil for them rather than his family and slowly watched his life's work deteriorate to an inoperable farm. He was lowered to having to scrounge for necessities for his family in the local dumps. He and all he had previously owned became the property of the communist government.

Communism does not allow private ownership; therefore, everything that was once his now belonged to the government. He lived in a hostile manmade prison, even though he was no longer behind bars. Socialism is a cancer that slowly eats away everything good and of value in the lives of its people. I saw firsthand the results of it in our lives and the people around us.

From the beginning of occupation, Igor's grandfather was sent from the main house on the land, which he and his family occupied for decades, to the servants' quarters. It was the anti-capitalistic tactic of the communists to prove that the working class should be the ruling class, so the rich had to be made low like the rest of the population. Although this did not add up, when the high officials of the communist party lived in the richest houses and had much more than the workers. They had special privileges everywhere, even in the food stores. The "people" had to stand in line for hours and sometimes days to get the smallest of necessities and many times when they arrived in the store, they found the shelves were barren. But the hierarchy had everything reserved ahead for them, whenever they needed it. The communist plan is a lie, and the saddest part is that the people didn't believe they could overpower the rulers of it in their nation. Consequently, they became subjects of this hypocritical rulership and were kept prisoners for forty long years. There is a time for peace a time for war (Eccles. 3:8). Just as God allowed the Israelites to wander in the wilderness for forty years (Num. 32:13). There is a time for everything (Eccles. 3:1).

Hopelessness and Discouragement = Post Communism

It was shocking to see what was left after communism in the beautiful country of Czechoslovakia. Everything around the people of this post-communist nation was grey, crumbling down, antiquated without hope, and yet they had to endure and adapt to their demise. During communism rule, many escaped. Almost as many as were in the country managed to escape for freedom, yet many died in the process and many were executed and imprisoned. My husband, Igor, escaped in 1965 to the country of Austria, where he was arrested and imprisoned for four months before they determined he had amnesty. With the help of Jesuit priests that he lived with for one year and Nelson Rockefeller, he was able to come to America. Thirty-five years later he learned it was also through a doctor friend of his father. His story is miraculous as well. I believe God had designated the exact time for his escape. He escaped from the Czechoslovak army in Prague with a false passport from a Frenchman he met at an art festival. Even though he escaped, the Frenchman was arrested when it was discovered that Igor had escaped with his passport. If Igor had gone back, he would have most likely been killed or imprisoned for life. It was not uncommon for the army to kill young soldiers in a firing squad execution, even on the very land we were to inherit. We received eye witness accounts from people in surrounding villages that reported seeing this take place. Again, God had a plan and nothing could stop that plan for Igor's escape and future. Even though at that time he had not yet met Jesus, God was leading him into the plan that was written in His book in Heaven before he was in his mother's womb (Ps. 139:16; Jer. 1:5).

The gates of hell will not prevail over the church (Matt. 16:18). God is not dead, as the communist would have liked the people to believe. Nothing can stop God. Not man, not disaster, not war, not famine, not any plan of the Enemy!

Igor did not yet know Jesus as his Savior, even though he was raised as a Christian in the Lutheran church. He knew about Jesus, but didn't have a personal relationship with Him; as I told you earlier, his conversion took place in America. I wonder sometimes if he had not come to America, would he have ever become a true Christian? Because he miraculously escaped from Czechoslovakia, I believe this was God's plan. I believe God answered the prayers of his praying grandparents and mother, who were practicing Christians, even during communism. When his father left the faith, his son received the blessings of those prayers. He told me about his maternal grandmother, who came home on Sundays from church to Tri Duby and sat in her kitchen and sang the Psalms the entire day. I have heard him singing the Psalms on some occasions as well. Don't tell me that parents and grandparents do not plant many seeds of faith in their children and grandchildren by their own demonstrations of faith leading to the salvation of their children and grandchildren's souls with their constant intercession for them. God hears the cries of our heart, and there is no one closer to us than our children and grandchildren. Keep praying mom and dad, grandma and grandpa; if you don't see the answer, it is on its way. God hears and answers in His time and His way. Maybe they will have to go to another land to find Jesus, but wherever and however God deems it to happen, let Him have full reins with your loved ones. The account of the miraculous conversion and deliverance of my son is another book in the future.

-15-
TRIALS OF THE NEW LIFE AND SANCTIFICATION

God uses each stage of our Christian walk for dying to self, so that He may live more in us. He allows trials of life to sanctify us, always leading us to our destiny. Since coming to Christ, I have experienced many trials along the way. Some of the most difficult trials began when we entered the enemy's territory in Czechoslovakia, where we found the communist mindset was still entrenched in the people and government officers we had to deal with almost daily. We went there to take back the territory the enemy of communism had stolen from Igor's grandfather. Very few people accomplished getting back all of their land without a big fight and going through miles of bureaucratic red tape. We thank God that we were one of the few who succeeded.

In America, by 1989 we had already transferred most of our data to databases on computers. But in Czechoslovakia, everything was still on paper, piles and piles of paper, some just stacked up in rooms from floor to ceiling, with no organization. Everything had to be stamped, sealed, and tied in ribbons, bound together in what looked like an ancient manuscript, with wax seals and ribbons binding it in a hard-cover book. Nothing was found or completed without piles of papers being shuffled and officially verified. It didn't take just one or two trips to an office; it took multiple visits of trying and agonizing attempts to find the right maps and official documents and then to have everything officially stamped again and again. It was a living nightmare for us as foreigners, who were not used to the antiquated system of leftover communism. Much to our chagrin, we quickly discovered this was not going to happen quickly, nor was it possible to speed it up. Our official slogan for things in those days was, "there are two speeds here, slow and slower." We simply had to accept it.

Unfortunately, the beautiful farm we were to inherit had been transformed into a thirty-five acre polluted garbage dump, with one barn restored, and the other ruins, nothing but walls. Igor's grandparent's house was nothing but a slab of concrete. Small parts of the ruins of the servant quarters where Igor's grandparents were exiled to when the communist army took over the land and the remainder of a grain silo still stood. Needless to say, this was not the inheritance we had hoped for, but thanks to a futile regime that ruined so many lives and an entire country, this is what we got. I want to insert a warning to the younger generations of America—you will not achieve free medicine, education, and other freebies from the government without paying for it somehow. The less government is involved in our lives the better, and the more freedom we will retain. Take it from my lesson learned firsthand from living and seeing what socialism and communism do to people and countries. Don't decide it is the way to go if you haven't really investigated and lived it.

After many trials and errors, we ended up going to the Slovak Congress, the highest government officials of the land, to get funding to clean up this piece of land that was officially considered one of the most highly polluted areas of land in the country. Igor envisioned going before the congress personally and making a plea for the help they actually legally owed us, but much to his surprise, upon going to the government office to file a complaint to the congress, he only found a little black window with a slot to hand a request through to someone he couldn't see. So, he wrote on a small piece of paper his request to have the land cleaned up, stating the truth, that this was a problem caused by the army that occupied it, therefore it was their responsibility to clean it up. Miraculously, within a short time we received word that the government accepted the responsibility for the cleanup and allocated millions of crowns for the work to be done. An act of God was performed considering this was not expected to happen...but God!

Multiple meetings with high army officials ensued in the days to come. They always started the meetings by setting a shot glass of Vodka in front of us at 8 a.m., which we always declined. We spent many sleepless nights at our little two-foot round kitchen table discussing, planning, and praying, asking God to move the obstacles out of the way for the work to be done. Those prayers were answered way beyond our imagination. Never underestimate what God can do; nothing is impossible for our big God. Time and time again God showed us His goodness and mercy.

This land was very prominent in Igor's memory as a place that was a beautiful working farm where he grew up spending many days of his childhood. I heard many stories of his childhood adventures there: falling into the vat of cream trying to just get a little taste; riding his bicycle to the local spa to bring back bottles of mineral water for his grandma; riding in a horse drawn sled in the winter under a large sheepskin blanket to church. Precious memories that could never be erased from his mind, even if what was once there was now just ruins.

A little history of the farm: It was formerly owned by a Count from the Austro Hungarian Empire, purchased by Igor's great-grandfather, as a gift to his son, Igor's grandfather; on the wall of one barn was a plaque with the date 1867. There was a lot of history on this land; it was being set free from occupation of the Russian army, the Czechoslovak army and now into the hands of a Slovak-American. What would become of it was yet to be seen.

The land of Tri Duby had been polluted by the Russian army with airplane fuel seeping from underground pipes into the underground waters, tons of garbage such as medical waste, and oil drums and mines and bombs covering thirty-five acres filled the land. Believe it or not, Igor and his partner carried the bombs off the property in the back of a Porsche to the airport across the street to be detonated. If we had not done it that way the whole operation would have stopped and who knows for how long. Praise God nothing ever happened! The new occupation was set in motion by God himself. It was time for Igor and I to have control of this land, because little did we know God had an imminent plan for it. His timing was crucial. How we stepped into God's timing for our destiny was yet to be revealed to us.

-16-

KNOWING JESUS MORE INTIMATELY AND DEEPLY

On this walk with God, I have realized that it's all about getting closer and closer to the One who loves me more than I can imagine, so I may know Him. I want to quote the words of Madame Jeanne Guyon, as a reminder of how we are to approach God to know Him more intimately and deeply.

This is an excerpt from her book "Experiencing the Depths of Jesus Christ," which was written in the late 1600s:

> *"Dear child of God, all your concepts of what God is like really amount to nothing. Do not try to imagine what God is like. Instead, simply believe in His presence. Never try to imagine what God will do. There is no way God will ever fit into your concepts. What then shall you do? Seek to behold Jesus Christ by looking to Him in your inmost being, in your spirit."*

Madame Guyon advocated praying the Scriptures as the first level of coming into God's presence. With deep contemplation in the Word of God and praying it back to God, one begins to sense God's presence. She says that after coming into His presence we can begin to understand who He is and experience the depths of His person as Paul longed to do (Phil. 3:10-11). Her point being that in order to know Christ we must enter into His presence first. Although, entering into His presence requires faith. We must believe He exists and is with us by faith not by sight (2 Cor. 5:7). If Christ has given each of us a measure of faith, then we have enough faith to go deeper. Just believe and do it.

I have found that God becomes real when we go through things that are impossible and we sincerely cry out to Him for help, then He answers us (Jer. 33:3). It is so amazing how He always sends the help we need and manages to get us through our own resistance to receive His help, even though it might not be how or when we want it. Thank God for His mercy and grace. Where would any of us be without it? It is so wonderful that He knows how far we can go away from Him and how much we need Him to find our way back. I just love how God works on our behalf. He doesn't have to do it, but He does it because of His great lovingkindness and His amazing grace.

God Meets Us Where We Are

God became very real to me in my wilderness experience in Slovakia. I can honestly say God is real to me because I have seen Him work and I have encountered Him through His Spirit and His Son Jesus Christ in my trials. It takes all three of them to satisfy a thirsty soul and a dying spirit. My spirit was renewed the day I met Jesus, and my soul began to be renewed in the sanctification process He is still taking me through. I am not where I want to be, but I am headed in that direction and I trust Him to get me there. There are days when I don't think I will ever get there, but I am still on my way. With my little bit of faith, I persevere through. The Apostle Paul said, "Brethren, I do not count myself to have apprehended; but one thing I do, forgetting those things which are behind and reaching forward to those things which are ahead. I press toward the goal for the prize of the upward call of God in Christ Jesus" (Phil. 3:13, 14 NKJV).

Leaving the Past Behind

There were plenty of things I had to put behind me to be able to move forward. The things of the past can either hold us back or propel us forward to do better and greater things. It is said, do not let your past define your future. Sadly, many people spend their entire life doing just that and never reach their destiny. My pains and heartbreaks of rejection and abandonment were many and being set apart in the wilderness was right where I needed to be, to allow those painful and difficult things to come up to the surface to be healed. When I could no longer hide behind a busy life, familiarity, comfort, or pride, I was vulnerable before God and man.

Philippians 3:10-11 (AMP) says, "[For my determined purpose is] that I may know Him [that I may progressively become more deeply and intimately acquainted with Him, perceiving and recognizing and understanding the wonders of His Person more strongly and more clearly], and that I may in that same way come to know the power outflowing from His resurrection [which it exerts over believers], that I may so share His sufferings as to be continually transformed [in spirit into His likeness even] to His death, [in the hope] 11 That if possible I may attain to the [spiritual and moral] resurrection [that lifts me] out from among the dead [even while in the body]."

This is my goal as it was the apostle Paul's and should be for all believers and true followers of Jesus. My determined purpose is to know Him and become so intimate and deeply in love with Him that nothing can tear me away from Him.

After going to Slovakia, my world was upside down; it was sort of like being caught in the undercurrent in the ocean and not knowing which way was up. While I still struggled with panic attacks and fears, God was digging deep into the chambers of my heart, where deep hidden places still needed to be uncovered. Let me define the heart in spiritual terms. It is the center of our being where the emotions, mind, and will reside. Our heart can be wicked and deceitful, although God desires to change our hearts and heal them.

We had some trying times with family members in Slovakia, people who did not understand who we were as Christians, and the government offices we had to deal with almost daily to accomplish our goal of retrieving all the land back. It was at times very stressful and tested our faith continually. Jesus gives us all a measure of faith according to scripture (Rom. 12:3); He is the author and finisher of our faith (Heb. 12:2); and the Holy Spirit gives us a gift of faith (1 Cor. 12:9). So, we have faith, but we still have to trust in the Lord and apply it.

Faith is a Requirement to Know Christ

Jesus Himself emphasized the importance of faith in Mark 11:22. He said, "Have faith in God." "Faith" in Greek (pistis) means conviction, confidence, trust, belief, reliance, trustworthiness, and persuasion. "It is the divinely implanted principle of inward confidence, assurance, trust, and reliance in God and all that He says" (New Spirit Filled Life Bible).

Our faith is born out of hearing the word of God, Romans 10:17 (AMP): "So faith comes by hearing [what is told], and what is heard comes by the preaching [of the message that came from the lips] of Christ (the Messiah Himself)." When we hear the word of God it brings understanding and revelation of the truth and faith is born by what we have heard and believed.

We are saved by grace through our faith. Ephesians 2:8 (AMP): "For it is by free grace (God's unmerited favor) that you are saved (delivered from judgment *and* made partakers of Christ's salvation) through [your] faith. And this [salvation] is not of yourselves [of your own doing, it came not through your own striving], but it is the gift of God"

Knowing Jesus is the Son of God, through His Word

God the Father Himself declared that Jesus was His Son, calling Him the Son of God (Matt. 3:17; 17:5; Mark 1:11; 9:7; Luke 3:22; 9:35).

Peter, the apostle, was there on the high mountain with Jesus, James, and John, when the Father spoke to them in an audible voice declaring, "This is My beloved Son, in whom I am well pleased. Hear Him!" (Matt. 17:5 NKJV)

Peter later declared to the people himself that Jesus was the Son of God. "For we did not follow cunningly devised fables when we made known to you the power and coming of our Lord Jesus Christ, but were eyewitnesses of His majesty. [17]For He received from God the Father honor and glory when such a voice came to Him from the Excellent Glory: "This is My beloved Son, in whom I am well pleased" (2 Peter 1:16,17 NKJV). He went on to say in verse 18, "And we heard this voice which came from heaven, when we were with Him on the holy mountain."

Peter's faith was born, because he heard the voice of God speak to Him. He saw His glory as a cloud on top of the mountain. The prophecy of Christ was personally experienced by him. This same experience has to happen to us as we hear the words which Jesus spoke when He came to earth; when we understand the many prophecies fulfilled in His life, death, and resurrection. We must hear from Him personally as Peter did, then we can believe.

I remember during an altar call at our church a young man from our youth group that was always getting in trouble and had a hard family life without a father, came to me after the service and told me God had touched him that night. I asked him how that happened. He said he literally felt a hand touch him on the back and when he turned around there was no one there. He realized it was God. He had never come to our regular church service before, but it took just that one night for God to become real to him. After he heard the word of God, he drew near to God and God drew near to him. Jesus became real to him and no one can take that from him. That is what had happened to me over and over and each time it happened my faith grew a little more and Jesus became closer to me.

Our faith comes by hearing Him and believing what we hear. Faith is a noun, believing is a verb. You must believe to have faith.

Knowing Christ by Faith Leads to Experiencing His Presence

"Practicing His Presence" by Brother Lawrence says, "In order to know God, we must often think of Him; and when we come to love Him, we shall then also think of Him often, for our heart will be with our treasure." In order to think of Him, we must first believe He exists. Some people will miss out entirely of everything God has for them, simply because they do not believe He exists.

Faith comes by hearing. One of the most certain proofs we have that God exists is His Word. We must read and hear the scriptures with our spirit eyes and ears open to know and believe in Jesus, our Redeemer. What follows is a demonstration of our faith. We will begin to think of Him, pray to Him, worship Him, and love Him with all our hearts, minds, and souls. Then we will begin to walk in righteousness, which is being a living epistle of Christ. It is said that Francis of Assisi said, "Share the Gospel at all times, if necessary, use words."

Job had a long discourse with God about who He was (Job 37-42). Finally, he said to God, "I had heard of You [only] by the hearing of the ear, but now my [spiritual] eye sees You" (Job. 42:5 AMP). This is what brought Job to repent and truly know God (42:6). When we encounter Jesus, it always leads us to repentance. He is the Light of the world and will expose the darkness in us, when we encounter Him.

God took me into the wilderness to hear His voice speak to me and guide me into the truth, by revealing the lies that I believed, and changing my mind by the cleansing and washing of His Holy Word. My faith grew little by little as I encountered my Savior and made Him the Lord and the Master of my life. When everything was stripped from me that I could choose to depend on, my next line of hope was Jesus. If I really believed His Word, then I had to act like it and trust Him with everything I had in me. He had to be all and all to me. My relationship had to become more than just a minimal encounter with Him; it had to become a fulltime encounter with every breath I took. What stood in the way had to be removed and I had to put Him first. I needed a heart change.

It is an awesome thing to be in the presence of the Lord and to hear His voice, but nothing happens from that experience unless we follow what He says to do. Sometimes He has to nudge us to get us to move in the direction He is sending us. My nudge came through pain and sorrows, anger and strife, reaching a point in my life that I could not deny any longer that I needed healing in my heart if I wanted to live the victorious life Christ died for. If I, as a mature Christian, have a need for my wounded heart to be healed, I wonder how many Christians are missing that life. Christ came to heal the brokenhearted. He read from Isaiah 61:1 in the temple; little did they know He was declaring this prophecy had been fulfilled in Him.

> *"The Spirit of the Lord GOD is upon Me; because the LORD has anointed Me to preach good tidings to the poor; he has sent Me to heal the broken-hearted, to proclaim liberty to the captives, and the opening of the prison to those who are bound"*
> *(Isaiah 61:1 NKJV).*

He came to do so much, but the one thing I want to focus

on is the healing of the brokenhearted. I had realized that after all these years of being a Christian my heart still needed healing, because it had been broken over and over in my life and is still being broken today but for the people who do not have a Savior. I was not free to receive the abundant life Jesus promised us (John 10:10). I was not victorious over the assaults of the devil through relationships or circumstances in my life. I was still carrying wounds and I only knew one thing, it had to come to an end, because Jesus came to earth for my victory and died and was resurrected to give me abundant life, to set me free, to restore my soul, and to heal my heart.

In my journey to the broken places of my heart, I realized that it was the problem with most Christians. They were missing what Jesus had promised, what He had died for, and the only thing they needed was a healed heart. They did not realize that the heart was the center of everything, and that we are at war for our hearts with Satan and His emissaries. Jesus came to heal hearts, because we all suffer from a heart problem that needs to be fixed. When I cried out to God for my own heart to be made whole and began to see that it was not just my heart He wanted to heal, but all broken hearts and that this was the missing link to a victorious life with Christ; it became my passion to experience my own healing and the healing of others.

-17-

THE HEART IS CENTRAL

If we begin to see the value and importance of our heart to our walk with God, it will begin our journey into freedom. God says a lot about our heart in His Word. It is a central matter to our relationship with Him and our relationship with others. I began to look at the Scriptures that declare the heart is an important matter to God.

Going back to the beginning of creation, we have to acknowledge that God has placed into man a perfect heart. After Adam and Eve were created, He looked at all He had created and said, *"it was very good."* Not just good, but *"very good"* (Gen. 1:31 NKJV). His greatest creation was man and woman and they had been completed and it was *"very good."* That tells us our hearts are good and we are good. Too many Christians get stuck on we are sinners saved by grace and believe they are still sinners the rest of their walk with God. That does not mean we still do not sin, even though we don't want to, but we have been given a new nature, the nature of the first Creation. We are a new creation in Christ, when we have received Christ into our hearts (2 Cor. 5:17).

Are you a new creation or are you still the old

unregenerate sinner that cannot get the victory in Christ that you were promised? Jesus said, "No one puts a piece of un-shrunk cloth on an old garment; for the patch pulls away from the garment, and the tear is made worse. Nor do they put new wine into old wineskins, or else the wineskins break, the wine is spilled, and the wineskins are ruined. But they put new wine into new wineskins, and both are preserved" (Matt. 9:16, 17 NKJV).

I was in a new environment in Slovakia, with new people, new culture, new beginnings were happening every day; God was formulating new beginnings in me as well. When I was taken from everything familiar to me, in a sense it was a strip-ping away of the old in my life. New wineskins were being formed. I would have to come clean with myself and God, I couldn't run to the old comforts I had before. There was time to think, pray, and seek God and the Lord began to do a work in me to bring up hidden things in my heart; He did it by mak-ing all my old ways inoperable. Nothing I knew worked where I was. I was humbled and helpless. Sometimes, God needs to allow us to become weak through circumstances, so His strength can be perfected in us (2 Cor. 12:9). I couldn't run to the phone and call my prayer partner, I couldn't go to my church and ask for prayer, I could not go out and work in my garden to release stress; all my ways of dealing with my pain or stress were inoperable in this strange land.

A new believer in Christ cannot keep the old heart and ex-pect Him to abide there. Jesus wants to abide in our hearts, not just come and visit from time to time, but He has to have a whole, new, healed place to abide. That is why He came to heal the brokenhearted, so He could come in and live. He knocks on the door of our hearts, and wants us to answer and welcome Him in, so He can commune and be intimate with us (Rev. 3:20). Someone once said that the door of our heart God is knocking on has a door knob only on the inside. In other words, it is up to us to open it; He just knocks.

To abide in Christ means to let Him stay and make habitation there. If you are moving into an old broken-down house, you first want to fix it up so you can live there. That is the same thing Jesus wants to do, He wants to fix up our old broken-down hearts, so He can live there. It is the central place for His residence. Everything comes back to this one place and flows out from there. The issues of life flow out of our heart. "Keep thy heart with all diligence; for out of it are the issues of life" (Proverbs 4:23). "To keep" your heart means to guard it, protect it from the assaults of the devil, abuses and hurts of life, because out of it comes our very life. "The issues of life" means the source of life itself comes from our heart. That is very big to a person who is wounded and brokenhearted. Are you starting to see how important it is to have a healed heart? Jesus didn't say He came to put a Band-Aid on the brokenhearted. You may have been putting Band-Aids over your heart for years, through alcohol, drugs, therapy, or some other source of comfort or escape that never gets to the root problem. Medication, a change of jobs, a marriage partner, a location, or even your looks will not help permanently. None of it works unless the Healer, Jesus Christ, comes in and takes over the wounded places and removes the lies and agreements we have made with the devil, about who you are in your new life in Christ. The King James version says, He came to "bind up." When a newborn baby comes into the world, we bind them in a swaddling clothe, so they feel secure like they were in their mother's womb. They need to know they are taken care of and secure, just as our heart needs to feel secure when we come to Christ. We need to know He is going to wrap His arms around us and protect, take care of, nurture, soothe, and fix every broken place from our fractured life experiences. He is our Healer.

How does He begin to do that? He lifts a veil from our eyes, so we can see the truth of who we are, so we can walk in freedom. "but whenever a person turns [in repentance and faith] to the Lord, the veil is taken away. Now the Lord is the Spirit, and where the Spirit of the Lord is, there is liberty [emancipation from bondage, true freedom] (2 Cor. 3:16, 17 AMP).

God Promises Us a New Heart

Ezekiel 36:26 declares the Israelites will be given a new heart and a new spirit, when the remnant will be with Christ. "A new heart I will give you and a new spirit will I put within you, and I will take away the stony heart out of your flesh and give you a heart of flesh" (AMP). The cleansing of their heart and spirit was necessary for them to walk in obedience to God, after they had failed to do so. God said he would do this for His name's sake, because they had profaned His name (Ezek. 36:23).

We are grafted into the tree of Israel, and given these same promises through Christ, the Messiah, who has already come (Rom. 11:17, 19). We live and reign with Him now when He lives in our hearts and we will live and reign with Him on the new earth as well, with our new glorified bodies, perfect hearts, and spirits. How then can we expect to have a perfect heart here? David was said to have a perfect heart in God's eyes. Did that mean he had no wounds or did not sin? Absolutely not, he sinned and was greatly wounded, but he always turned back to God for his healing. The anointing of God on our lives, as with David, is often infused with pain, suffering, trials, and tests. God uses them as a barometer of our hearts. How we handle what we go through tells God a lot about our hearts. We need to receive healing in our hearts and know that God has everything that was ever done or said to us that has become a wound covered by His blood. Healing is available to all believers, but we must quickly come to Him as David did. David's psalms tell us how He came to the Lord for the healing from his broken heart. "The humble shall see this and be glad; And you who seek God, your hearts shall live" (Ps. 69:32 NKJV).

We need the Holy Spirit to guide us and empower us, to purify our hearts through faith in Christ. Peter spoke to his Jewish brothers concerning the Gentiles he was sent to: "So God, who knows the heart, acknowledged them by giving them the Holy Spirit, just as He did to us, and made no distinction between us and them, purifying their hearts by faith" (Acts 15:8, 9). The gentiles were uncircumcised; God accepted them as well, so that all could have a purified heart and all brokenness could be healed, when they came to Jesus and received the Holy Spirit.

God was making me who He wanted me to be. My job was to understand how much He loved me and allow Him to live in me in all my shortcomings, wounds, brokenness, and pain, fully trusting that He would make me into a new wineskin and fill me with His Spirit to fulfill my destiny.

Don't discount what God is doing in your heart and life through the trials and pain you may be going through right now. He has a great ending to your story. It's written in the book about you in Heaven (Ps. 139:16), and He wants more than anything for you to fulfill it. We all need His help to get to the end of the book. Let Him work in you however He needs to accomplish His will. This has been a big part of my journey into intimacy with Jesus, may He give you the grace you need to withstand the attacks of the Enemy and be stronger in His power and might of the Holy Spirit.

-18-

ANGEL ENCOUNTERS

I knew about angels, because the Bible tells us about these created beings of God that act as messengers for Him, warring for Him and ministering to His servants, as they did to Jesus while He agonized in prayer, sweating blood in the Garden of Gethsemane. The angel Gabriel came to Mary to announce to her the birth of her son, Jesus Christ, who would be the Messiah (Luke 1:30, 31). Michael the Archangel came to Daniel's rescue, warring with the Prince of Persia, so his prayers could be answered for Israel (Dan. 10:12, 13).

One night while lying in bed in our apartment in Bratislava, I was awakened out of a sleep to a bright light standing next to my bed. It took the form of a being of light that appeared to have wings and long flowing hair. I could not see the details, but just the form as a white, bright, shimmering light. In every account of someone encountering an angel in the Bible, they were paralyzed with fear until the angel said, "Do not fear, I am sent by God." That is exactly what happened to me. I was terrified and felt paralyzed unable to move or speak. Then I heard those words, "Do not fear, I am sent by God." My heart was pounding; I thought I would have another panic attack, but thank God it didn't happen. I was also so mesmerized by the presence of this amazing being, which was actually sent by God to give me a message, that I was frozen. I cannot reveal what that message was because it was personal and I have still not seen it completely fulfilled, but it is in the making, even as I write these words twenty-five years later.

Sometime after that, I was awakened again in the night and sensed the presence of the power and glory of God in the room. I was again fearful. If we don't have the fear of God in us, we do not know Him. God is to be feared, because He is the most amazing and awesome power we will ever encounter. He has the power to destroy, to create, to heal, to raise the dead, to change the impossible things in our lives and in the universes. He is God in heaven, and He can do whatever He pleases (Ps. 115:3).

Suddenly I heard the Holy Spirit's still small voice speak to me and tell me He was giving me a new heart. Then I saw in a vision a hand reach toward me and resting in it was what looked like a perfect heart of flesh. My old heart of stone with all its wounds and scars was being replaced by the hand of God. I began to cry and tell the Lord how much I loved Him and a peace came over me that washed all my fears away, and then I went into a deep sleep. I sincerely believe that it was part of the transforming process God was taking me through. He revealed Himself to me as a caring, loving and powerful God, who wanted to speak to me personally and change me into that new creation in Christ, according to His promise to all who believe. These encounters are as clear today in my mind as the day they happened over twenty-five years ago. I also had two more encounters with angels in Central Slovakia some years later in our apartment there, and saw an angel as a human on our land at Tri Duby. Angels are created beings that God uses to help us, to protect us, to send us a message from Him. I am so grateful for the encounters I have had and pray I will have more. Above all else, I was never more determined to know God and to be intimately and deeply in love with Him. Sometimes he uses angels to reveal Himself to us. Some people may not believe what I have just shared, but it doesn't matter; it was my experience and I believe it! I pray you will have those encounters too. No one is exempt from experiencing God in a deeper way, if you only desire it and begin to seek Him more. He just might use an angel to do it.

-19-
TURNING UP THE REFINING FIRE

When a silversmith refines silver, he heats the precious metal so hot that it melts, and in its liquid form the dross or the bad stuff floats to the top so he can skim it off. He does this over and over. He knows it is purified when he can look into it and see His reflection. The refining fire of God comes in whatever form is necessary to bring up the dross in us, to purify us and make us more and more like Jesus. I am grateful that I had trials with fire that brought the hidden things to the surface and exchanged them for deep encounters with God, because they changed me forever.

In the process of knowing God and how much He loves us, we encounter who we are, and many times we don't like what we see—the dross gets ugly. That was true for me. I hate to admit it but I was full of pride and thought I could do everything myself outside of God's or anyone else's help. What a mistake that is, because it will be put to test in life's trials. As the word of God cleanses our character, we will become a finished vessel for God's glory and honor. My heart was deceitful and wicked, my mind needed to be changed, my will wasn't aligned with God's, and my focus was not completely on Him. The refining with fire was going to get even hotter.

God doesn't have anything to do with all the bad things that happen to people. Some things we bring on ourselves through wrong choices, some are demonic attacks, and because we live in a fallen world bad things happen, but God will turn them around for our good (Rom. 8:28). It certainly wasn't what God wanted to happen. After the sin of Adam and Eve, God gave evil permission to work in the world. Bad things do happen to good Christian people, because we are the arch enemy of the devil and sometimes, we reap what we sow from our past. Sometimes it seems so unfair that bad people do not have as much bad happen to them as good people, but their day will come, if not here after they leave this world. God is sovereign. Scripture says the sun shines on the good and the evil and it rains upon the just and the unjust (Matt. 5:45). God doesn't see the things that we call bad as we do. He sees everything as an opportunity for us to grow and draw near to Him, to trust Him for help, and receive His lovingkindness towards us. All sickness comes from the devil or our fallen nature, whether we caused it ourselves or not. Everything good comes from God, and bad comes from the devil (James 1:17). God certainly doesn't cause the bad things, but He is with us through them all.

> *"Yea, though I walk through the valley of the*
> *shadow of death, I will fear no evil; For You are*
> *with me; Your rod and Your staff they comfort me"*
> *(Ps. 23:4 NKJV).*

God sees our trials as opportunities to fine tune us, to temper us, to change our character to be made more into His image, for which we were created, to be more and more in His likeness. Many of these things that come against us are created by our own reprobate selves, some by the demons around us, and some by circumstances out of our control. Yet in all these things God is still there, He is still sovereign, and still the same as He always was. He still promises to make good out of all that tries to destroy us, because we love Him and are called for His purpose (Rom. 8:28).

In the process of the work we had to do in Slovakia, God was not only accomplishing miraculously the things we needed to get done concerning the lands, He was also working on our character to change us into His image. Lighting fires around us, teaching us to put them out the way He would do it, and giving us courage and grace to go through every trial. I can honestly say He gave me a new heart; a heart of compassion that turned my eyes off of myself onto people all around me who needed Jesus.

A missionary is sent, but God has to do the work through them wherever He sends them. If I was sent to show people Jesus, they needed to see Jesus *in* me, and that is what needed to be revealed in me through the refining fire of adversity. This was my task, letting Him change me, learning to work *from* His love, not *for* His love. I was loved and I needed to know how much He loved me, and it didn't matter who I was before or what garbage I still had in me to be cleansed and purified. His love remained, it was always there, and will remain forever. I needed a revelation of how much God loved me so I could fulfill the first commandment, "You shall love the Lord your God with all your heart, with all your soul, and with all your mind" (Matt. 22:37 NKJV).

-20-

TO KNOW GOD LOVES YOU
AND TO LOVE HIM BACK

I will say it again: one of the most important things we experience in Christianity is that God loves us. I had to grow into this truth. The Word of God tells us that God loves us (John 3:16), that God is love (1 John 4:8), and yet because of my brokenness and uncertainty that anybody loved me, it was difficult to understand that God loved me. People often get very frustrated with others, because they treat them badly and say they love them, but are far from showing it. Only when I realized no one was really able to truly love until they were reconnected to God, who is love, did I understand it. That is to have a true born again relationship with God to be given His spirit and be reconciled back to Him, after being born into the world with the sin of Adam.

On that day in the church that I met Jesus, it was just the first step to being born again. I was being drawn by His spirit and step by step being changed and made new, by knowing Him and accepting Him as my Lord and Savior. I was determined to follow Him, and He put a hunger in me for Him and His word, so I was being transformed day by day. As I accepted God's love for me and grew closer and closer to Him, I was then able to love Him back and love others with His compassion, mercy, and grace, which were free gifts to me and to all who believe. I am still learning this today. Daily I realize His great love for me, and it brings me to tears over and over as I worship Him and enter into His presence.

Knowing how much God loves us also allows us to fulfill the second most important commandment of God, "You shall love your neighbor as yourself" (Matt. 22:39). Jesus said, "This is My commandment, that you love one another as I have loved you" (John 15:12 NKJV).

When we know the love of God and can love Him and love others, we have fulfilled our purpose. Everything we do from there will be according to God's will, as though He was doing it through us; it is no longer us who live but He who lives in us (Gal. 2:20). We can't work for God's love, to try to prove we love Him or receive His approval and love, but we can only do good works if we know He loves us. Ultimately, it is not us doing anything, but Him working through us. Jesus said in John 15:5 that we can do nothing without Him. We can then freely love Him and others and our works will come from a place of love, from the heart of God to others. The compassion of God is what has to flow through us for others to see Jesus in us. From His love and compassion, He healed the sick, He fed the hungry multitudes, and He raised the dead. I prayed this prayer, *"Lord, do not only send me, but change my heart into your heart that I might love the way you do."*

Loving the Unlovable

Loving the unlovable has been the common denominator in

our ministry to the poor, the needy, the outcast, the mentally ill, the depressed, the brokenhearted, the addicted, the sick, the imprisoned, and the helpless. In all our tasks as land stewards, we encountered every kind of person you could imagine. God brought them into our life one after the other to minister to and to love the way Jesus did. When His love is in you, it comes easy, but people make it hard, because they do not always accept the love or change in the process the way we want them to. I often said, life would be great if it weren't for people, with a laugh after, of course. We are the problem most of the time, and that is why we need Jesus.

When I think of loving the unlovable, I often think of a particular Gypsy woman named Sylvia, who tested me more than anyone. One day I was sitting at the park in Central Slovakia where we lived at that time. I had my Bible in hand, while my son Michael was playing, when God gave me a very good lesson on loving the unlovable. A tiny little Gypsy woman with dark eyes, hair, and skin sheepishly came up to sit by me. I detected she was somewhat shy and fearful.

I was reading my Bible and watching my five-year-old son Michael playing on the playground equipment. In our small conversation with my broken Slovak, I found out her name was Sylvia and she had a little boy around four-years-old with her, who was her grandson named Tino. She wouldn't let him go from her side. The little boy wanted to play with the other kids, but she wouldn't let him. She asked me what I was reading. I told her "The Bible." In my broken Slovak I spoke to her about Jesus, and she responded right away. Almost instantly she started to cry and tell me she didn't have anything to feed her grandson, Tino. I could see that she was a very hurting person. I didn't know the whole story, but I could see that she needed God's love. I urged her to let Tino go play with my son Michael, and finally she reluctantly did. Then I asked her if I could pray for her. She cried again as I prayed for her; I knew the Holy Spirit had touched her. Little did I know where this first meeting would lead in our relationship; God was about to teach me about His agape love. Sometimes God sends someone who the world considers unlovable in our path to teach us how to love others the way He loves us.

Sylvia was an unlovable person according to society and the world's view. She had all the cards stacked against her. First complaint was she was a Gypsy, the scum of the earth in Europe. The Gypsies were known as thieves, liars, beggars, stupid, dirty, uneducated, you name it they had the label. She was also a woman, a widow, single grandparent, and unemployed. There was not much of a reason to like her or love her, yet that love of God was exactly what she needed.

She asked me if I could give her a Bible, so I invited her to my house to get one the next day. I told her where we lived and she came by the next day for her Bible. Looking back, I probably set myself up by doing that, but God knew what He was doing, even if I didn't. I could see she was very troubled and didn't quite know how to handle little Tino, so I began to be her mentor spiritually and life coach for the simple things of life. The needs of this simple, castaway, child-like woman were very interesting and unique. I didn't know much about the Gypsy culture, but Sylvia was about to teach me all I needed to know. Some of the people from my church did not like the fact that I invited her to church, because the Gypsy people were shunned and not trusted. They were called *cygans* in Slovak or liars in English. The best job they could hope to get was sweeping the street or digging a ditch. It certainly didn't help them to stop stealing, because they couldn't find work to make a living for their families.

There were also skin-heads who would attempt to kill or injure them. They threatened them by throwing rocks in their houses and breaking windows and basically caused them to be afraid to the point they would stay away from the city. One day, when I was walking with Sylvia to the store, there were two very large athletic looking skin-heads approaching us, and she became very frightened and I told her don't fear God is with us. They immediately began to call her names and throw cursing words at her, even though she was walking right beside me. Adrenaline kicked in and I immediately became like a mama bear and went into their faces, even though one guy was six-foot-three, I told them to stop. It had to be the Holy Spirit, because I have no idea how I was able to speak to them in Slovak so clearly. I think they were so shocked they didn't know what to do and stopped dead in their tracks and got quiet. Sylvia looked at me after and had a big smile on her face and was so amazed that I had stood up for her. It was probably the first time anyone had ever stood up for her in her life. Her self-esteem was so low that she could not even look you in the eyes when she talked. Sylvia needed to see how much God loved her through my actions and behavior toward her. I just love how God steps in where we leave off.

There were many things I needed to help Sylvia with; she was similar to a child when it came to life skills. In some of our kitchen table talks, I found out her own father was in prison for murdering her mother and burning her body in a house. Who knows what kind of abuse Sylvia and her family suffered at home.

Our daily life lessons continued and she learned to care for Tino with simple discipline technics, so he wouldn't become an unruly child and overrule her authority. Her son, Tino's father, wouldn't help her with him or pay her bills, so I helped her with electric bills a few times. She was so grateful that she insisted on helping me somehow, so we decided she could come to my house once a week to clean and help me in whatever way I needed help, and she did it faithfully.

In our Bible reading sessions, Sylvia accepted Jesus as her Savior, and she hungered for the Word. She arrived at my house like clockwork almost every day. I would hear her voice at the bottom of the stairs to our apartment calling my name in her sweet little voice, *Lindushka* (Lin dush' kah), an endearing way to say my name. My true test was when I heard her calling my name and I have to confess there were many times when I wished she was not coming that day, but instead I had to put on the Jesus loves you face and heart and let Him love her through me. She was clearly my challenge in loving the way Jesus did. To this day I am so grateful for her.

She loved her Bible so much she slept with it and many times spilled coffee on it, but she kept it close and read it daily. I was so excited that she loved Jesus. We did go through some trials that she had to repent for and admit her lies and return some money she took under false pretenses; it was bound to happen sooner or later. Through these trials we taught her the ways of God, and she submitted in humility to them. There was a sign of humility in her that was so amazing to see.

Several years later, when I came back to Slovakia, I saw

her on the street. She had a job sweeping the street and her son was now taking care of her grandson. These were some of the things we prayed for and God answered. Some years later I found out that she passed away. Though I was sad to hear this news, I was so happy that I had been able to lead her to Jesus. I know I will meet her again one day in heaven. Difficult unlovable people need Jesus and if we don't love them and tell them, who will?

> *"And how shall they preach unless they are sent? As it is written: How beautiful are the feet of those who preach the gospel of peace, who bring glad tidings of good things!" (Romans 10:15 NKJV).*

There were many others we had the opportunity to lead to Jesus. Like the Gypsy boy who was a dwarf and taken from his family at six years old, when the Communist institutionalized him because of his handicap. He was considered an outcast first because he was handicapped and secondly because he was a Gypsy. The world labeled him and limited his life completely.

The Communist kept all homeless, mentally and physically afflicted people out of society in institutions, so everything looked good on the outside to the world. He suffered much abuse while there, such as being locked in a very small room for weeks at a time. When communism fell, this young man received word that he was free to leave because he was eighteen by then. Before he knew this, he climbed out of the window one night to attend an evangelization meeting in the Czech Republic and met Jesus. I met him in a church in Bratislava and we became his spiritual parents. For over a year he lived with us, until we left to come home to America. There were "unlovables" of all walks of life that we were led to disciple and lead to Jesus. What an amazing life it is to serve the Lord!

Who is God putting in your path to love like Jesus loves, to share the gospel with, and disciple in their new life in Christ?

-21-

COMPLETE IN ME A GOOD WORK LORD

*"I pray with great faith for you, because I'm fully
convinced that the One who began this glorious
work in you will faithfully continue the process of
maturing you and will put his finishing touches to it
until the unveiling of our Lord Jesus Christ!"
(Phil. 1:6 TPT).*

Coming to Slovakia was the beginning of going through the refining fire, to become the vessel for God's glory I was called to be. All the trials we went through to get the land back for Igor's mom were just a taste of what was yet to come. As I said, his mom had a written list of everything down to a pitchfork. Because of this list, the value of those items gave us the right to have the same value back in equipment for the farm. After about four years of hard work, going from office to office to get all the papers in order to transfer documents, to get restitution for property and items taken from Igor's grandfather, we received back a tractor, plows, trucks, a bulldozer, a combine, fertilizer for our fields, seed for crops, and many other things to replace all on that list.

117

It was amazing to see that after the land was cleared of thirty-five acres of pollution and garbage, we could actually farm on it. We planted wheat, corn, and the most memorable crop of all, potatoes. Tons of potatoes were harvested, after all the manure that was carried by the dump truck loads to our land by the Coop as restitution payment. My smelly, fun job was to count the truck loads as they weighed at the Agriculture Coop. I had my clipboard and tallied the weight and number of truck loads.

A most interesting adventure occurred during the process of all that manure loading and dumping. At the end of the day, Igor and I drove to Tri Duby to assess the manure piles on the fields and as we counted them, much to our surprise there were two truckloads missing! We recounted and sure enough, they were missing. Immediately we put on our Sherlock Holmes and Dr. Watson hats and did an investigation, as to where the two missing truckloads of manure were. Evidence must be found! We were shocked when we located two perfect piles of fresh manure in the trucker's garden. As any investigator would do, I got out my trusty 35mm camera and took photographs as evidence in case of a court case in the future. In all seriousness, we were very surprised, but it was also very funny to be looking for manure piles. We laughingly decided apparently his garden needed fertilizing. It got even funnier, because Igor used a card from the ministry of war that was given to him as a calling card to confront him about his "misplacing" the fertilizer in his garden.

During our investigation that evening, we talked to some of his employees who confirmed the theft, because they drove the trucks and dumped them in his garden. It was nice that they confessed so easily. Probably because they didn't think they did anything wrong.

Our plan was to surprise him early in the morning and demand he bring the stolen property back the next day. We knocked on the door, and he was still in bed, but finally came to the balcony in his pajamas and spoke to Igor, who was holding the Ministry of War calling card in hand. When we gave him our proof of the manure sitting in his garden, he relented and admitted his guilt. We demanded that he show up the following morning to deliver the two missing truckloads of God-given fertilizer to our property.

Much to our surprise he showed up just as we had asked to deliver the missing smelly cargo at nine o'clock sharp, as planned. I watched the conversation a few yards away between Igor and the admitted thief just imagining what they were saying. Igor told me later when he reminded him he was stealing from us and could be arrested, he said, "If that is the case, most Slovaks would be in jail." In other words, it was a common practice to see something you needed and take it, because it belonged to the government and in their minds that would not be a problem to steal from the government. Nobody understood ownership, and independent landowners were not known or acknowledged at all; the rewards of a communist system. To him the manure was just being taken from the governmental Coop, not from a person.

In conversations with local friends, we learned that factories produced well, but a large portion of the materials went home with the workers, because they needed it. With low paying jobs, they certainly couldn't afford to buy the supplies they needed, so why not just take it? It was not uncommon to see a house with a store front entrance. Guess where they worked? In a factory that made storefront materials. It was a different way of living than the word of God taught; of course, they didn't know that because most had no word of God, so the atheistic immoral state of mind in a large part of the population bred immoral behavior.

Sin was not a problem because it was not even known to be sin to an atheist. Even though we can know something is good or bad, there still isn't any reason to not do it, other than I might get caught and have a punishment. It is a shallow way of controlling people in society that usually doesn't work, because they will still try to get away with whatever they can in hopes they won't get caught, because they know nothing about eternal consequences.

For the person who thinks they go to heaven if they are good, they might have more reason to do good, but they still are lacking in understanding as to why we are to do good and to fear God, or receive eternal consequences. God knew we wouldn't be able to keep all His commandments, so He graciously sent His only begotten Son, Jesus, to suffer and shed His blood for all our sins, past, present and future, with repentance.

Therefore, we have a reason to follow the law, because God commands us to follow His Word and He is the ultimate authority. Without Him, we are on our own and doing our own thing, not His will but ours and that never fulfills God's plan for our lives. Jesus said he was not from this world, and when we come to Him neither are we of this world.

There are three things that deter us from living a righteous life as John the apostle wrote. When we live according to the world, we live by the "the lust of the flesh, the lust of the eyes, and the pride of life" (1 John 2:16). Paul wrote that "the flesh lusts against the Spirit" (Gal. 5:16), and he admonished us to walk in the Spirit and not fulfill the lusts of the flesh. Let's face it, the flesh is our enemy. We are always warring against it, whether in food and drink, sexual desires, or wanting to satisfy it constantly with something outside of God. The war is on, when we surrender our lives to Jesus, but the good news is that He empowers us to overcome the flesh with His Spirit.

The desire to do good is not enough to be able to walk under the power of the Spirit. We need the power of God in us to overcome the flesh. Nothing can be done by our flesh; it must be submitted to God. I remember the days, when I strived to be good, it never worked. Sin of the flesh is always crouching at the door just waiting for us to fail in our weakness. Looking back, I had convinced myself by the lies I believed, that I was good, but not until I met Jesus did He show me that I had nothing good in me. I learned I was saved by grace through my faith in Jesus and not by my own good works (Eph. 2:8). The song "Amazing Grace" certainly describes it well. I was a wretch, once lost and now found, blind but now I see. He opens our eyes to see things as they really are.

Back to the stolen manure, it was returned and we were very happy and he was baffled as to why we thought it was such a problem. His plan would have been to go to the Coop and tell them we were short two truckloads, and they would have probably given us more. After all, one thing there is plenty of where there are cows is manure.

As Christians, we are to have the mind of Christ, so Christian thinking is quite different than that of the world. We are commanded by God to obey the laws of man and God. When we don't, something happens in our spirit called conviction and we cannot live without repenting and doing the right thing. Living in sin will torment you if you have received the Holy Spirit after salvation. Jesus left the earth, but He left the Holy Spirit, who would convict us of our sin (John 16:8). This is the best barometer we can have in life. The Holy Spirit keeps us in check at all times; our job is to listen and obey. Conviction leads to repentance, which is a change of mind and heart that causes us to leave our sin behind to turn and go the other way, the right way.

Potatoes to Evangelization

All those truckloads of fertilizer brought an abundant crop of potatoes on our land. We had so many potatoes that we filled our enormous barn with tons of them. Because of the large crop, we needed to find a lot of help to harvest them. But there was a shortage of harvesters. It was not the best weather for harvesting because of a lot of rain, so we couldn't begin until November, which was very late. Everyone was trying to harvest at the same time, and we were dependent on Coop machinery to turn the potatoes up from the ground, so we could have hired workers to pick them up and bag them.

We finally got the machines to come and managed to hire Gypsies to come to our land and do the harvest. Igor went to an apartment building in a nearby village, stood outside and yelled out, "Does anyone want to harvest some potatoes and get paid every day?" They came running like dogs chasing a cat! Well, that was unheard of for the Gypsy people to have work they actually got paid for the same day or at all. The next day the truck picked them up and we began to harvest.

We let the workers take home as many potatoes as they could carry and they got paid their wages at the end of every day. They walked away with big bags filled to the top, so heavy they could hardly carry them, so we took them home in the truck every night loaded down. We had no idea how we would pay them every day, but by the grace of God, He provided just in time.

It was an amazing operation, especially since we had never done anything like this before. Some of the workers were bagging, some were loading on the trucks, and some were unloading in the barns. It was a very fruitful operation, daily producing and providing for our income and the poor at the same time. We slowly got to know the workers in our daily encounters, and every day I made huge bowls of American-style potato salad with Sylvia's help and served them lunch with sausage cooked on the open fire on a stick. They were quite amazed at how they were treated compared to the humiliating treatment they were used to, with very little pay. When the light of Christ shines out of God's people, others see it and are drawn to it. Darkness flees in the light and light also exposes the darkness.

In Luke 1:78-79, it speaks of Jesus as the Dayspring that has come to visit us; to give light to those who sit in darkness and the shadow of death; to guide our feet into the way of peace.

The first day of our ten-day harvest was very successful. The rain had stopped, after a lot of prayers, and everyone went home happy with a large overflowing bag of potatoes. Much to our surprise, after such a successful day with our workers, during the night thieves came to the barn with a truck and loaded it up with potatoes and took them God knows where. Not being used to the commonality of theft, we were very shocked and displeased.

The next day Igor began to ask some of the workers questions about it, and before long the thieves were exposed right amongst our workers. We kept it quiet until we had our fire pit lunch. While we were eating, those who had stolen the potatoes the night before were politely but firmly asked to leave the property. They were given every opportunity to confess and to return the stolen goods, but they chose not to, so we ask them to leave. The others saw what happened, and we didn't have any problems with theft after that.

God gives us innovative ideas to lead people to Himself. On the way to the fields a few days into the harvest I had an idea pop into my head to take photos of the workers, so I got some film for my 35mm camera and began to take pictures of them all; no digital cameras or fancy cell phones in those days. They were very excited about it and kept asking me every day when they could see the photos. I promised them each a photograph of their own. There was a reason God put that thought into my mind, which I would find out later. In the meantime, the harvest continued, and we began to pray for them and ask God to draw them to Himself. As I said before, the harvest was delayed into November, so it was extraordinarily late because of rain, but the rain completely ceased while we were harvesting for ten days. God was so involved in this whole operation that even the weather obeyed. It was so glorious to watch the miracles unfold every day.

November is my birthday month and it fell on the last day

of harvest, so I got a true Gypsy celebration. They grabbed my feet and my arms and swung me back and forth singing a Gypsy birthday song. It was such a joy to become part of these people's lives. Because God is faithful to meet all our needs, the very first day after we completed the harvest it began to rain again. It never ceases to amaze me how God is in every detail of our lives. We should never feel that God is not interested in our little problems, small or big. Every part of our lives is important to our Creator, Father God.

Go and Tell Them the Good News

After the harvest, I promised the workers we would bring the photographs to them when they were developed. This whole thing was a set-up from God for us to share the gospel and lead people to Jesus. Jesus' last words to His disciples were, "Go therefore and make disciples of all the nations baptizing them in the name of the Father and of the Son and of the Holy Spirit" (Matt. 28:19 NKJV).

The whole time we were harvesting we were speaking to them about Jesus and several young men got saved. There were about ten young men from that apartment building that were sniffing glue. One young man named Peter received Jesus as his Savior and quit the glue sniffing, and his testimony led all the others to stop sniffing glue and receive Jesus too. That wasn't all that God did—later He even closed down the glue factory. God was moving in their lives, and we were watching it all unfold, because we went where He sent us, to a strange land I did not know to encounter people with the same need as all people—Jesus Christ.

Several weeks had passed since the harvest, and it came

time to take the photos to the people, so we made arrangements with Peter to come to his parents' apartment to meet with the people and distribute the pictures. The apartment building was dilapidated, the windows were broken out, and I was a little afraid to get in the elevator, but the people were kind and open to receive us. They had heard from others about God, such as Jehovah Witnesses, and were curious about what we believed, so the door was open to share Jesus with them. Some wanted to hear, and others did not. When we discovered the need of one family, we offered to help them get a washing machine, but they refused it because they thought we were trying to force them to believe what we believed. Nevertheless, God opened a door to go into their homes and tell them the gospel and pray with them on a weekly basis, just by taking some photographs. God knows what we need to do, if we will just listen. I later found out the reason it was so important to them to get the photographs of themselves was that they had never had a picture taken of themselves before. Some lifelong friends came from those relationships that we are still in contact with today. Most importantly, there were lives redeemed and set free in those encounters that we will meet in heaven one day and live eternally with.

-22-

TIME TO RETURN HOME TO AMERICA

It seems that all good things usually come to an end. After we received the land back and all the restitution was completed, we were planning to build a house on Tri Duby where Igor grew up making many fond memories. But first we needed to return home to get Michael enrolled in a homeschool program in New York, so I could continue homeschooling him upon returning to Slovakia. At that time, we didn't know for certain when we would be returning, but it was our desire for the future. After three years, I did not want to leave Slovakia, because it became our home and we had many good friends and family there that would be difficult to leave behind. My life was completely changed by this experience and I was no longer who I used to be, nor did I have the same desires and needs before going there. I learned to let go of everything and hold nothing except Jesus dear to me. Without Him I could not live and never wanted to for the rest of my life. When Abraham was called out of his home country of Ur, he never returned and his life was forever changed. My life was drastically changed by leaving my home country, and little did I know that my life was getting ready to be changed even more, and this time it was going to be a deeper overhaul.

Back to America

I resisted leaving my new home in a foreign land, even though Igor was saying we had to leave. Ironically, he was attached to America and I was attached to Slovakia; go figure. Until I heard from the Lord through His Word, I resisted submitting to leaving. But one day while praying and reading the Bible, the Lord spoke to my spirit and I knew it was time to return and finish unfinished things in my life. I really don't remember what scripture He spoke to my spirit with, but I had a peace after that and knew it was the right thing to do. Many times we go on our own will or on our feelings, but if we seek God for direction and wait on Him it will always be the right time and way.

Off to America we went, two duffle bags a backpack and Michael's trusty companion, Wrinkles, a Shar Pei dog puppet that went everywhere with us and had made multiple trips across the ocean. He was entertainment for Michael on the long trips and like a part of our family.

Since we sold everything in America and left everything behind in Slovakia, we really had nothing but our clothes, so we stayed with a dear friend and went on with life. It was a very difficult time for me, because I felt like I had no purpose. I was accustomed to being around people, ministering everywhere I went, in schools, in our home, our church, and amongst the many people we encountered. I immediately went into a very dry wilderness place, sitting in the basement of someone else's house in New York, and became depressed.

My life seemed useless for God as I homeschooled Michael, who was seven years old by then. I felt I did nothing for the kingdom of God, except to go to my little country church in the hills of New York on Sundays. I felt lost and dead inside, missing my life in Slovakia and close encounters with the Lord.

I could not understand why God wanted me to be back in America in the basement of the home of two little old ladies, with my son, doing what felt like nothing for the kingdom of God but teaching him every day. I virtually felt like I was on another planet and the enemy was attacking my mind day and night, while depression was winning more than not. It was becoming more difficult and complicated every day, and I could not see one good thing happening in my life. I also came back to the reality of my broken family relationships and all the past hurts and wounds of my failed life before Christ. My life appeared to be useless and hopeless at this point. I even came to the point one day that I was ready to throw away my Bible and all things I had connected to Christianity. I was depressed, angry, hopeless, and close to completely giving up. One day out of my despair I threw everything into a box and said, "I am finished!" It was Michael who reminded me about Jesus and all we believed and taught him to believe. The faith of a child is priceless and powerful.

The environment we were living in was full of tension, arguments, and in my eyes, depressing. Inside, I was screaming for change, but had no way to make a change. My thoughts were overpowering me, questioning my very existence. Why couldn't I just go back to where we were happy and fulfilled doing God's will in our lives? Why did we have to come back to this bottomless pit, which seemed like a living hell to me. On top of that, I was going through early menopause, which escalated my situation a thousand percent.

Even though I was not walking in the peace and joy of the Lord at that time, one night what I thought was an angel appeared to me in that basement it looked like a light and then I heard the Lord say, "Everything that looks like light is not light." I realized that I was being harassed and tormented in my mind by demons, who wanted to drag me under, after all I had experienced with God in Slovakia. The enemy literally wanted me to give up on God and stop ever doing mission work again. The next day I unpacked the box with all my Bibles and Christian reminders and restarted by focus. We have to take steps toward God and He will always meet us where we are.

My Calling/Homeschool Mom

Every day I did the best I could to teach Michael what he needed to learn for the New York school curriculum, and I did a Christian teaching with the Bible every day. We each took turns reading the Bible. He would read a chapter, and I would read a chapter. When we got to the New Testament in Romans, Michael turned to me and said with tears in his eyes, "Mom, I want Jesus to forgive my sins." I was so amazed and thankful for that most precious moment of our lives together. It made all that I thought was useless turn into the most amazing worthwhile experience of being a mom and homeschool teacher I could ever dream of. I felt like I had purpose again, it was not a useless life after all. God has a ministry for every human being He has created; no one is useless or without purpose. Whether you are a mom or dad, lawyer, doctor, teacher, student, or friend to someone, you can be used by God to change lives by your testimony and sharing the love of Jesus. No life is without purpose.

During that time in the basement of a house that didn't belong to me, with very little direction or understanding of what I was going to do with the rest of my life, I was being awakened even more to how much I needed to draw near to God and wait upon Him.

-23-

WILDERNESS EXPERIENCE

The wilderness is where the Israelites wandered for forty years, never making it out of their endless troubles to enter the Promised Land. I certainly didn't want to stay in the wilderness for forty years; I had already wasted forty-five years of my life with wrong decisions away from God and now which way do I go? Day by day I was challenged by the people around me and my questioning and wavering understanding of what God wanted me to do with my life. I only know that I was in the fire, the heat was being turned up, and I needed to meet the fourth man in the fire to be saved. You may have heard the story of Shadrach, Meshach and Abednego, who were thrown into the fiery furnace to die. The furnace had been heated up seven times hotter to instantly turn them to ashes, but when King Nebuchadnezzar looked into the furnace, he saw them walking about without a scorch or burn on their bodies. The most amazing thing was that there was a fourth man walking in the fire with them, who was their Savior. The King described him as looking like the "Son of God" (Dan. 3:25). They refused to bow to worship the King and burning to death in the furnace was their sentence, but God honored their refusal to bow to a man and to worship Him alone and sent His Son to save their lives. The One that was sent was the only One that can save us. His name is Jesus. I needed to encounter the only One, who could save me from the fires of adversity and emptiness in my life, Jesus Christ. I knew Him already and certainly accepted Him as my Savior years before, but God wanted me to know Him more.

> *"When you walk through the fire, you shall not be*
> *burned, nor shall the flame scorch you"*
> *(Is. 43:2b NKJV).*

Fire burns, flames scorch, but Jesus stands between us and everything that tries to destroy us. He came to save! Adversity was upon me, emotions were attempting to take me into a realm of darkness I couldn't get out of, but the Light was much brighter and illuminated everything that darkness was trying to cover up. What needed to be exposed in my heart and ultimately healed was seeping to the surface under duress and it was an ugly experience I would have rather not gone through, but it was necessary and good. As the old saying says, "no pain, no gain." Pain sometimes causes us to be strengthened. A bodybuilder will tell you that when their muscles are in pain after heavy lifting, they have been torn and will heal stronger than they were before.

Before going to Slovakia, before coming to Christ, my life was in a downward spiral, and there didn't seem to be any way out. It reminds me of Joseph being thrown into the pit by his brothers having no way out. He cried and cried, but no one answered, no one came to help, until he was ultimately sold into slavery. I felt alone and without help for my heart was deeply wounded from divorces and abuse by past marriages, abandonment and rejection. I think it really didn't affect me as much when I was an ocean away, but the closer I came to my home the harder it was to run from the pain. Igor was good at seeing what I needed to do, but I was more reluctant and wanted to hide as much as I could from my pain. I didn't understand that I couldn't hide from it; that would just be a temporary way to avoid dealing with it, which was not going to make it better but actually make it worse.

Many people are hurt, abandoned and rejected in this life. That's why we need Jesus who came to heal the brokenhearted (Is. 61:1). So many things can happen in this life that are unexpected, some self-inflicted, or put on us by the destructive ways of others. Life sucks sometimes, but we can't let that stop us or destroy us from living a life of purpose and peace.

I lived on a roller coaster of emotions, because most of my focus was on myself and what I was feeling or not feeling. Life was an emotional up and down experience that seemed to never end, hopeless, depressing and lacking in every way. It baffled me as to how I could go from being so happy in Slovakia to such misery in America. I did not understand it. If our happiness is determined by what is happening to us, it will never be stable; it will always go up and down according to our good or bad experiences. That is not the way Jesus told us this life should be. He said He came to give us peace and an abundant life. I was far from that, but determined to still follow Jesus and experience what He had died and suffered for on the cross. He did say it was finished, before He breathed His last breath. The finished work He came to do was to bring the kingdom of God to earth and give mankind a way out of sin and death. He needed a church, the body of Christ, to carry on after He left. The timeline for our lives is set in motion the moment we are created in our mother's womb. He knew us before and has a great plan for our lives. As scripture says, our lives are written in the books in heaven. (Ps. 139:16) It's our destiny waiting to be fulfilled.

As in the case of Jeremiah the young prophet, God said to him, "Before I formed you in the womb I knew you; Before you were born I sanctified you; I ordained you a prophet to the nations" (Jer. 1:5). That means before God created Jeremiah, He knew him. Before he was born, while still in the womb, God sanctified him or dedicated him and set him apart to be a prophet. His future and destiny were already laid out for him. Now that God had called him, he complained to God, "Ah, Lord God! Behold, I cannot speak, for I am a youth" (Jer. 1:6). When God told him his destiny, he didn't want to accept it and wanted to make excuses for not being able to do it. If God ordained it and created him to do this, there is no way that running from it or refusing to do it would have a good out-come.

So why do we run from our destiny sometimes and find ourselves in a pit unable to get out without God's help? God always wants us to do more than we can even imagine, so that we know that it is Him who did it. He gets the glory and we stay humble.

Jeremiah was given a very difficult job, to deliver unpleas-ant messages to the sinful nation of Israel. He was just a youth and could not imagine being able do the job of a man. God told him, "Do not say, 'I am a youth,' For you shall go to all to whom I send you, And whatever I command you, you shall speak. Do not be afraid of their faces, For I am with you to deliver you, says the LORD" (Jer. 1:7,8).

With God all things are possible when we trust in Him and His power, not our own. We can fulfill our destiny, if we trust God. Jeremiah trusted God, even though he might have had doubts and fears and faced much adversity, He had to believe that the voice he heard was God and there was a purpose and plan for his life.

"For I know the thoughts that I think toward you, says the LORD, thoughts of peace and not of evil, to give you a future and a hope" (Jer. 29:11 NKJV).

I had to learn to trust God's plan. Like Jeremiah, God had a plan for my life and this wasn't the end for me, but perhaps it was making me ready for what I was called to do and I hadn't seen the whole picture yet. Again, it's a walk by faith, not by sight. I had to trust in Him, even when I couldn't see anything happening. A word from the Lord clarified this to me years later, "Faith is not trust, it's already done; just trust. Trust comes through relationship with the Lord...knowing and believing is a part of it. Trust initiates faith."

-24-

JOURNEY TO FORGIVENESS

The road to finding the calling and purpose that God had for me meant doing some things I didn't want to do. God used my faith-filled husband, Igor, to help me walk on the path to freedom. Igor decided we needed to get a van and travel down the East coast and eventually go to see my family in Kansas. To him it was a necessary thing for the issues with my family to be solved. He was right, but I was fighting against it all the way, purely based on fear of more rejection. The picture that fear painted in my mind was a no-win situation. I felt that because Igor had never met my dad, he didn't know how serious this was. Nevertheless, we got the van and began our journey, prepared to camp all the way down the East coast. We definitely took the long way around, from New York to Key West up to Tennessee, Missouri, and then to Kansas, my home state.

When the time came for us to be in Kansas, we stayed at my sister's house 300 miles from my hometown, where my parents lived. Much to my surprise, they came to see us there. The anticipation of them coming made me sick to my stomach from the fear of what my father's reaction would be to me, after seven years of not speaking to him because he wanted it that way. In my sinful old life, I made some very bad decisions and it lead to this separation. The day finally came when they arrived and we went outside to greet them. We said hello, but mostly Igor spoke to them and they met Michael, their grandson, for the first time. Believe me; any attention taken away from me was much appreciated. I literally wanted to just melt away into the earth, so no one would see me at all. Igor was very excited to meet them and reached out to them, but my dad didn't say much to me and rather avoided me. Let's just say the tension was very thick in the air.

When I went to bed that night, I did not sleep the whole night and was actually very sick to my stomach from nervousness. No one can tell me stress and fear don't cause you to be sick. All night long I kept hearing the still small voice of the Holy Spirit in my mind telling me I needed to apologize and ask my dad to forgive me. I thought to myself, for what? He should apologize to me. Pride raised its ugly head again. The scriptures that taught about forgiveness kept ringing in my head, reminding me of what I had to do like it or not.

Jesus said forgive seventy times seven; in other words, forgive no matter what (Matt. 18:22). Your heavenly Father will not forgive your trespasses, if you do not forgive those who trespass against you (Matt. 6:14, 15). I don't think I slept one hour all night. When it was finally light, I got up and went upstairs to the kitchen and realized my sister and family were all gone. There was only my family and my dad and mom in the house. Much to my dismay, in the kitchen sat my dad reading the newspaper and drinking coffee, while Michael and Igor slept and my mom was bathing. It was just me and dad in the kitchen. Reckoning time had arrived. If that wasn't a setup from God, I don't know what was. No matter how hard I tried to get out of facing him I had to. I was about to do the hardest thing I ever had to do, to forgive him when he didn't deserve it in my eyes. I said good morning and then he started to get up and leave the room, but I heard the Holy Spirit say, "Stop him before he leaves." I said, "Dad, can I talk to you?" He said, "Sure." We went into the living room, both feeling very awkward we sat down. I began by saying or should I say the Holy Spirit started talking for me, "Dad I am very sorry if I have hurt you in any way. I never meant to hurt you. I made some bad decisions in the past and I hope you will forgive me." He gave me his opinion about my misguided decisions briefly, but immediately said, we will just have to put this behind us. We hugged and he patted me on the back and we said I love you. The ice was broken, the wall was torn down, healing could begin and it did. It was the greatest miracle in my life to have that wall broken down. It couldn't have happened without the Holy Spirit empowering me and Jesus giving me the grace to forgive and ask for forgiveness, even when I didn't see that I needed to. The truth is I was just as guilty, by my actions, lies, and deceptions that I was not willing to admit to at the time. God is so gracious and forgiving of us, when we don't deserve it, all the more reason for us to be forgiving when those who offend us don't deserve it either.

Forgiveness, even when it doesn't make sense, is one of the most powerful weapons we can use against the Enemy. After all, Jesus forgave us, and we didn't deserve it. His mercy and grace has saved us. Jesus said follow me; that means do what I do. The chains that fell off of me that day made a difference in my life that nothing else could have done. The next twenty-five years with my dad and mom were the best years we ever had together. We drew closer and closer because of the love of Jesus and the forgiveness of Jesus in my life. It was His heart that turned everything around in my life. He gave me a new heart, a heart of flesh, and took away my wounded, stony heart forever. This was a very big step to making my life better and the new creation in Christ to be revealed in me and my destiny fulfilled.

When God uncovers the hidden things in our heart and soul, we may not like what it requires of us, but it is always the best thing we can do. Obedience is better than sacrifice. Jesus said that if we obey His commands, we love Him (John 14:21). Obedience is the key to demonstrating our love for Jesus. My obedience to go to see my father and do what the Holy Spirit and the word of God was commanding me to do brought freedom from the sin of unforgiveness to me.

Sometimes we are looking at the other person and expecting them to change, and we overlook what God is asking us to do. A man of God once taught me that to hold onto unforgiveness was like having a ball and chain around your neck, which is a very heavy burden we don't need to carry. Forgiveness breaks that chain and sets us free to accomplish God's will in our lives. I have seen people healed instantly, delivered from pain physical and emotional, and doors that were closed opened through forgiveness. Forgiveness is a very big deal. Don't delay it in your life and take just a few minutes right now to ask the Lord for the grace to forgive anyone that you may be holding things against, so the chains of the sin or unforgiveness can be broken off of you and you can walk free.

Sanctification Continues

God's cleansing work continued for me when I returned back to New York. We moved to a different place with a different friend, but the environment was more demonic than we expected. I felt so trapped and did not know where to go or what to do. The only thing I was able to do was pray, so I got together often with my friend and prayer partner, Joyce, to pray. Before returning to Slovakia another sin in my life had to be dealt with—being unmarried legally and living with Igor.

One day, I visited my prayer partner, a dear friend who prayed with me through many trials in my life. We were in her house upstairs praying, and I began to hear from the Holy Spirit, *you need to confess your sin and be healed.* I knew in my spirit exactly what the Holy Spirit was talking about. So, I confessed to my friend that Igor and I were not legally married. If we confess a sin, the next step is to change what we are doing. "Metanoeo" in Greek, "repent" in English, means a change of mind, which leads to a change in actions and purpose. In my old unregenerate mind I thought it was ok, because we had stood in front of God and stated our vows, which I believed God honored, but there are also the laws of the state to fulfill. The next step was to realize I needed to change this situation by getting legally married. When I returned home, I talked to Igor about it and asked him if we could get married legally but he refused, because he truly believed we were already married. His mind was made up and there was no changing it, until God, through the Holy Spirit, would speak to him, as He did me. Igor had not received that revelation and conviction like I did yet, so I had to do the hard thing and take a more drastic step to be obedient to what God was telling me to do. My only option was to move out. I remembered a friend from church had told me if I ever needed a place to stay to call her, so I did and she said sure come over and I have a room for you and Michael. With difficulty we packed up our few belongings and loaded them in the van and Igor took us to her house. I was hoping on the way he would change his mind, but he didn't.

It was a very difficult thing to do after seven years together, but I was determined to follow God and His ways over my own desires, as painful and difficult as it was. It was the determination of the Holy Spirit in me that allowed me to take this drastic step for complete freedom from this sin. The consequences of our sin sometimes follow us and make the transition stage to salvation and freedom in Christ seem like it's not worth it, but in the end it is always worth it, especially when we see God do supernatural things that we could not even imagine on our behalf. The stages of sanctification or being set apart for the Lord are not always easy, but necessary to become who we are in Christ. If we are Christians, we can't just be hearers of the Word, but our lives must reflect it. James wrote, "But be doers of the word, and not hearers only, deceiving yourselves" (James 1:22 NKJV).

Over the one month period that we were separated, I hung up on Igor's phone calls multiple times, because he kept insisting I come back, and he would not submit to marrying me. It was not an easy thing to do, but I was determined to be obedient to the Lord and what He wanted me to do. With persistence, I continued to pray for his heart and mind to be changed, until one day he called with a completely different attitude and asked me to call a friend of his that he had run into in New

York City that changed his perspective on everything. She was a woman friend, whom he witnessed to years ago and helped to get out of homosexuality to become a Christian. She had just graduated from seminary and was an ordained pastor; talk about a transformation by God. And what are the odds of him seeing her, after many years away from New York City? I believe God was answering my prayers. We serve a supernatural God, who does things we cannot even imagine.

After we hung up, I called her and she told me what happened in her conversation with Igor about me leaving him and wanting to get legally married. She simply asked him, "Do you love her and want her to be your wife?" He answered, "Yes." She replied, "Then why don't you marry her?" All of a sudden, a light went on in his mind and it was a yes for him after that. It was settled, and we began to make our plans for a civil wedding at the court house with two witnesses, our son, three friends, a borrowed dress; shoes, and even the wedding ring was borrowed. We were poor at the time, but rich in Christ. In those days we didn't have cell phones, internet, or a computer; life was a lot simpler and I liked it a lot better in many respects.

Igor had kept asking me if I was going back to Slovakia with him, when he went to New York City to buy airline tickets to go back and finish our work. But I repeatedly said no because we weren't married. Now that we were getting married, I could say "yes" to returning. God's plan was in motion; all I had to do was be obedient when the steps presented themselves.

-25-

BAPTISM OF SUFFERING

In August of 1998, Igor went back to Slovakia one week after we got married and purchased tickets for me to come in a month. After arrival back to our old home, we made our abode on the land of Tri Duby in a small portable house that we intended to live in until we completed the house we were building. There was a silo that had potential to be a house, so we began to bring water lines and electric lines in to start building. It was fun designing it and thinking about what it would be like to live on this beautiful piece of land in our own home. In the meantime, we made a kitchen and bathroom in one end of the barn, which had been rebuilt, and slept in the portable house that we made our bedroom and living quarters, until the house was done. It appeared as though we were moving forward into the place God had called us.

Igor was doing some harvesting for farmers around the area, with the help of his distant cousin, and we were having a great time. They literally had to rebuild the engine on the combine before harvest started, but there was something they needed to fix and the only place to get the part was in the mountains a few hours away. It was a rainy day. I was homeschooling Michael, and Igor and his cousin came into the room to say goodbye. Michael wanted to go with them, but I said no, he had to do his schoolwork. They were laughing and joking as they went out the door and got into the little red Ford Fiesta and took off.

The day went by and I was expecting Igor to be home before dark, but he wasn't home and I was getting worried. With no phone it was impossible for me to know if he was ok. After waiting for the entire evening, Michael and I finally went to bed. Then there was a knock on my door while I was still lying in bed awake, unable to sleep. I was afraid to open it, but I asked who it was and I realized it was Igor's cousin's family. They told me there had been an accident, and I needed to come with them. I kept asking if Igor was ok, and they wouldn't tell me. The language barrier didn't make it any easier. I was in tears by now and insisting that someone tell me something. They took me to his cousin's house and called the hospital. I spoke with someone there that spoke some English. Everything is a blur after that. I just knew that Igor was in very bad condition, but I didn't know anything else. His cousin had died instantly in the crash. It was a very difficult time. Immediately the family of his cousin started to accuse Igor for causing the accident because he was driving the car. I don't know how they could have determined that with no police investigation yet.

It was the beginning of one of the worst nightmares of our lives. Every dream was shattered. Here we were ready to finally make a home there, and the Enemy immediately came to kill and destroy. They wanted me to sleep at their house that night, but I couldn't sleep, I just stayed up and prayed all night in bed next to Michael, for Igor and for the family of his deceased cousin.

The next day I called a friend of ours to pick me up and take me to get some clothes. It was a very uncomfortable situation for me to be in the house of a man that died in a car that my husband was driving, and the family was now blaming him for their loved one's death. Michael and I went to our friends to stay that night. Many friends came to our aid to help us and pray for us both in Slovakia and America in the days ahead.

It was over twenty-four hours before Igor's brother could come from west Slovakia and take us to see him in the hospital, two hours away in the mountains. I found out he was in a coma, had a hole drilled in his head to monitor his brain, broken ribs and sternum from the seat belt. Thank God he had one on, because his cousin didn't and died instantly. Unfortunately, he always refused to wear one. Igor also had a broken wrist and leg and was on a breathing machine, which led to a serious lung infection. His prognosis was bleak. The doctors could not tell us whether he would wake up or in what condition he would be, if he did. When someone is in a coma, they are in the closest stage to death. The brain is asleep and the rest of the body is as well. It was a time to pray like never before.

Eventually Igor's father, the founder of plastic surgery in Czechoslovakia, pulled some strings and got him moved to a better hospital closer to where we lived, and the doctors there literally saved his life. Had he stayed where he was, I don't know if he would still be here. The head doctor-surgeon of the hospital where he was moved was so angry when he saw his condition upon arrival, that he made some very strong phone calls to his colleagues in the other hospital. I was fortunate that this doctor could speak English and was very highly spoken of and the head of all surgeons in the country. He actually advised me to file a lawsuit for negligence against the other hospital, but of course I never did that, with too many other things to deal with.

Upon arrival at the new hospital, Igor immediately was taken into surgery to have a metal rod put in his leg; he was cleaned up, and then after several days in ICU, he was transferred to a special hospital across town for infections because he contracted a severe lung infection in the first hospital. This hospital was quarantined from the public. Only I could go to see him and Michael or anyone else had to look at him outside through a window. It was very difficult and dark days for us all, including Michael.

In the first hospital, while he was in a coma, I would only be able to call to see how he was every day. It also required me to go to many offices and even to Austria to try to get a special visa to stay in the country while he was in the hospital. It was very complicated, but the good news was that I was his legal wife and that gave me the privilege to apply for a spouse visa of a native born Slovak. Praise the Lord. God knew a more important reason why I needed to be his legal wife. You mean to tell me God knew all along this would happen? Many people get mad at God when bad things happen, especially to good people. It's a question we all can ask, because it just seems so unfair. We cannot judge people by bad things happening. You have probably heard the statement, "life is not fair and bad things happen to good people." It says in the Bible that it rains on the just and the unjust. God loves all people and wants all to be saved. Suffering comes to good and bad people and sometimes it looks like the most evil suffer the least. I will be the first to say so, after all I have been through and many others around me that have suffered severely and certainly didn't deserve it.

Recently we lost a dear little boy from our church, named Cameron, who had suffered his entire eleven years with the dreaded disease of Muscular Dystrophy, then needed a heart transplant at age five, and had curvature of the spine that just grew worse and worse. Combined with the MD it caused him to not be able to breathe, eventually leading to a tracheotomy. He lived his last year and a few months with much suffering and pain to just be alive. Finally, he was freed from his ravaged physical body and given his new Heavenly body, free of pain and disease and more alive than ever with Jesus. The only way to understand the suffering a person like Cameron was going through is to know that because of sin in the world, we are still going to experience disease and sickness. He didn't deserve it, he wasn't a bad kid being punished, he was born with this as many handicapped children are. Even though we prayed diligently, fasted, warred every way we knew how for Cameron's healing, we didn't see it happen, as we had asked. Many times, his life was saved to go on with our prayers, but still his body finally couldn't take what he was undergoing anymore and he went to be with the Lord. This was the real miracle of healing he received, free of all pain and suffering, running, rejoicing with the angels, doing whatever he couldn't do here and so much more. We thank God that during his sickness he accepted Jesus as his Savior and understood and was very interested in learning things about God and eternal life. I prayed with him often and we read the Bible together and did a little Bible study when we could. He wanted to know about death and what happens after because he knew he was headed there. We are so thankful for his life and the impact he had on so many people. His life was finished here, even though it was not the right time to all who loved him.

In the midst of suffering and sickness and disease we have to remember God is not punishing us, but it is still part of the curse of Adam and Eve's sin in the garden. I do have to add that some disease comes from our own neglect of our bodies, so death can come early. God doesn't want us to suffer, but to walk in divine health and to be healed according to His Word when sickness does come. The solution is Jesus, sent to save us all and give us the promise of healing and the gift of healing others through the wonder working power of the Holy Spirit. The Lord gave us the power to heal and be healed through the stripes on His back and His blood shed for us that delivered us from the curse of sin and death. This beautiful child received his healing in heaven rather than earth, even though we prayed for years for his healing to happen here. I never stopped believing that he would receive his miracle. One night when I was crying out to the Lord for his healing, He spoke to my heart and mind, "I am about to give him the greatest healing of all, to live eternally with me in heaven, where there is no sickness." I don't understand completely, but I trust that the Lord's plan is the best and this child had completed what was written in the book in Heaven about him. He impacted many people including me with his sickness and suffering, He was my hero, and I never take my health for granted and was very touched by the courage and love I saw in him. He lived through so much suffering and loved Jesus so much and now is free indeed in Christ.

We don't understand fully God's ways or thoughts. "For as the heavens are higher than the earth, So are My ways higher than your ways, And My thoughts than your thoughts" (Isa. 55:9 NKJV).

There is a baptism that we as followers of Jesus must undergo, if we are truly His followers. No one likes it, but it is a part of being a Christian. Number one, the devil hates us and wants to destroy us; number two, we must die to ourselves and suffering; trials and tests help us to do just that. We can get mad at God, blame God, hate God, but it doesn't change the fact that we will go through suffering and God will use it for our good if we love Him and are called for His purpose.

Romans 8:28 (NKJV) says, "And we know that all things work together for good to those who love God, to those who are the called according to His purpose."

Concerning Igor's accident, I believe God knew what we were going to go through and was covering us every step of the way. There is a time and a season for everything, a time to be born, a time to die, and it was not Igor's time to die. On the eighth day after the accident when I called the hospital, he had responded to the nurses a little bit. I was elated. The interesting thing was that three days before he responded for the first time, Michael and I were on the bus returning from Vienna, Austria, seated next to a certain Jewish husband and wife. They overheard me talking to Michael in English and struck up a conversation with us asking what I was doing in Slovakia. I told them about Igor's accident and my difficult situation, so they said they would pray for him at their grandfather's grave and wrote his name down. I learned that they were going to her great, great, great grandfather's grave in Bratislava to pray. I was familiar with this grave. Her grandfather was Rabbi Chatam Sofer (1762-1839), Bratislava's most famous rabbi. He was world renowned for his comments on the Talmud and Tora and the founder of conservative Bratislava's yeshiva (religious school). Jews from around the world came to his grave to pray.

The couple could speak English but no Slovak and didn't know where they were going, so I was able to help them get money exchanged and a taxi to help them get to the grave and back to their bus to the airport in Vienna to return to Israel that same day. What were the chances of this happening? Again, I will remind you that God has everything about our lives already written in a book in Heaven. It is all in His time and His way.

This was a God-incidence for sure, and on the third day after their prayers, Igor awoke from his coma. If you don't know the significance of blessing the Jews, please learn, because they are God's chosen people and He said if we bless the Jews we will be blessed; if we curse the Jews, we will be cursed.

After God spoke to Abraham and told him to get out of his country, away from his family, to a land that He would show him, He said, "I will make you a nation; I will bless you and make your name great; and you shall be a blessing. I will bless those who bless you, and curse those who curse you; and in you all the families of the earth shall be blessed" (Gen. 12:1-3 NKJV). This was a covenant that Abraham had with God and still stands today. That is why when America blesses Israel we are blessed, and when we curse Israel, we are cursed.

You can see it throughout the history of our nation. When you vote for leaders, vote for those who support Israel and stand on the word of God in their policies, especially concerning saving the unborn and children from sex-trafficking. Our nation is weighing in the balance in the midst of a spiritual war, and God's people play a major part in deciding the outcome. My husband and I have always supported Israel, and we see the rewards of it in our lives.

When I left the Jewish couple in their taxi, they said to me, God sent you as a blessing to us. And I said, no He sent you as a blessing to me. I believe Igor woke from his coma as a part of the blessing. The doctor had no hope, said he could be a vegetable for the rest of his life, and we didn't know how long that would be. We sat in shock in the room with the doctor as she told us the very bad prognosis. But God had a better plan, and His plan always surpasses ours and is better than anything we could ever imagine.

Igor was moved to the infection hospital, and even though he had awakened from the coma, he was very lost in his mind yet. He didn't know me or where he was or what had happened. He had hallucinations, was tied down to the bed, constantly trying to chew his cast on his wrist off and was coughing up phlegm and had large quantities of phlegm suctioned from his lung infection daily that no medication would touch. He was in a very bad condition, with a tracheotomy and still could not remember me for many weeks, but there was at least hope of recovery.

The night after coming back from the hospital for the first visit with him, as I lay awake my tears began to flow and I heard the Lord say, not in an audible voice, but in my mind,

"Why are you upset?" I answered, "I don't know what is going to happen to Igor." His reply was, "Read My Word to him and it will heal him." I wasn't expecting to hear that, but from then on, a supernatural faith rose up in me. I never cried another tear, while God's grace sustained and carried me through the days and months ahead. One minute with God can change everything.

From that time forward I read God's word over Igor's broken body, as people were praying around the world, including the Jewish couple I met on the bus. God did exactly what He said He would; His word healed him. On the eighth day, Igor awoke from the coma, three days after the Jewish couple prayed. After about two months, he asked me if I had a Bible that he could read, and I left him unrestrained with his Bible in hand reading. It was a true miracle. Three months later he was able to come home and slowly regained his strength and memory. God's word is truth and does not return void. Igor is living proof of it.

-26-

GOD SPEAKS AGAIN

Two months of hospital visits with Igor were not easy with an eight-year-old boy and two bus rides to get to the hospital. The bus did not run on Sundays, and we had to hitchhike into town. On one Sunday we were waiting at the bus stop to thumb a ride to town when I saw Michael sitting on the bench with his head down. I thought there was something wrong with him, and when I asked if he was ok, he said I am praying for a ride. Immediately a car pulled up and stopped, the faith of a child at work. It was an old friend we hadn't seen since we came back to Slovakia, and he didn't know about Igor's accident, so he immediately took us to the hospital to see him. Igor didn't really remember him, but it was a blessing to have contact with him again and he began to help me as much as he could, to get the apartment on our property ready for Igor to come home in the future. God was watching out for us at every turn and never left us without the help we needed.

Although staying on the land alone with Michael was not advised by most people, I had faith that God was with us. He proved it to me many times over. The second night after the accident, we were staying with our friends in town, and I had a very strong feeling that I needed to go home because I knew in my spirit something was not right there. The next day when we got home, I found the gate on the entrance to the main road was down and the padlock was off. Then I went to the building where we stored all our equipment and the iron gate was down, the lock was off, and it was the same on the other buildings, but amazingly nothing was stolen. As I was reading the Bible that night, I felt there was something wrong and the Lord assured me, through His word that He was there and nothing would be gone. I had to trust He was there watching out for us. After that I was never afraid to be there by myself, even though I was constantly told by family and friends not to stay there alone. I knew I wasn't alone; there were angels camped all around us and we were safe in the arms of our Savior.

I shall not fear but have courage because the Lord my God goes with me wherever I go (Joshua 1:9). He goes before me and sends angel armies all around me that fight for me. "For He shall give His angels charge over you, to keep you in all your ways" (Psalm 91:11).

Michael was called into the ministry, I believe, at eight years old. Every day we read the Bible together, prayed, and sang hymns together. The first day after Igor's accident, when we went to see him at the hospital, it was very traumatic for Michael as a child to know his dad was in a terrible accident. When we got home that night, we were sitting in the kitchen and Michael looked very sad, so I asked him what he was feeling. He said he was sad because he didn't know if Igor would be ok. I said let's pray and sing some songs to Jesus, so we did, and after singing the Holy Spirit came in the room and Michael began to prophesy. He said, "Igor will not smoke anymore when he wakes up, and he will be going into churches to tell people how God healed him." He is a true prophet because all of this came to pass. Then Michael said, "Mom that wasn't me talking, was it." I said it was the Holy Spirit using you to prophesy. He asked me, do you think I will be a pastor someday? Michael is a fulltime missionary today, after many long hard battles, but God began to call him at a young age. Our children have a destiny just like we do, and it is important to raise them with the word of God to help them to find their calling and fulfill their destiny.

The days after Igor's accident turned into months. Nearly two months had gone by, and he was still not healed from the lung infection. He had to be fed through a tube in his stomach and still had the trach to breathe. The hospital wanted to send him home, but we had no home to bring him to yet. I began to work on getting the money to build a temporary apartment at the end of the barn where our kitchen and bathroom were. It was already started and would just require adding a couple more rooms to give us a living room and bedroom. Our friend that picked us up that day at the bus stop helped us get things going and my brother-in-law helped to finance it. We thank God for the help we had; He was continually doing miracles on our behalf.

There are many things we can't understand in life, and to question the reasons God allows especially bad things to happen is really not an option for a true believer. Which is not to say we can't ask God questions, by all means ask all you want; He wants to listen and answer. It's part of prayer, a two way conversation with Him. When the sudden-lies happen we just have to say Lord help me, I don't know what to do or the reason for all this, but I accept what you are doing is for my good. One day you're fine and the next you're not. You have what you need, and in a few moments, you've lost everything, disaster strikes, tornadoes come, floods come, accidents happen, and yet God is still on the throne and He still loves us and cares for us. It really comes down to how connected to God we are that these things don't destroy us, but cause us to crawl into the secret place and find our refuge and rest there.

> *He who dwells in the secret place of the Most High shall abide under the shadow of the Almighty. I will say of the LORD, "He is my refuge and my fortress; My God, in Him I will trust" (Ps. 91:1-2 NKJV).*

We have to encourage ourselves like David did when his enemies were surrounding him, or when Jehoshaphat was surrounded by all the armies that could easily destroy all of Israel. What did he do, but call the people to fast and pray, tell the worshippers to get warmed up, because they were going to go before the army and sing praises to the Lord and not to be afraid because the battle wasn't theirs but God's (2 Chron. 20:15). Three armies were brought down right before their eyes and they never had to fight. God is a miracle working God. We believed for a miracle for Igor, and God was answering.

God was speaking to me in many ways all the way through this post-accident period, but one day a month into it, while standing on our little porch looking out across the fields, I heard that still small voice of the Holy Spirit say the most unusual thing, *"Buy health insurance, you will need it."* I ignored it the first time, but after I kept hearing it in my head over and over, I realized God was wanting me to do something and I better listen. A big issue for Igor was that we didn't have health insurance, and of course after an accident you can't buy it. After multiple times hearing this message, I noticed a building in town that had the word insurance in Slovak on it, so I went in to ask if it was possible to buy health insurance for a foreigner. I found out that I could, but I needed a hundred dollars to buy it for one month for myself and Michael. At the time I didn't have the money with me, so I had to leave it for another day. Not too many days after, I was almost hit by a car coming around a corner when I crossed the street; it narrowly missed me by a few inches. I was alerted again to buy health insurance. This time I went to buy it for one month, which was all I could afford at the time. Now, why God would say this to me, I was about to find out.

After two and a half months in the hospital, Igor was slowly improving, and Michael and I were still going to see him almost every day. It was very hard and tiring for us, but we did it out of love and concern for his care. The hospital was financially going bankrupt, so I had to buy his medicine and diapers; mix him food to feed him every day through the tube in his stomach; read the Bible to him; brush his teeth; give him a pedicure; shave him; and pray over him. It was a labor of love to care for him. The infection was still not gone and the medicine had to be shipped from Austria to help him.

Igor's accident was on September 3, 1998, and on November 19, 1998, ten days after my 50th birthday, I found out why I needed health insurance. The workers were busily building the apartment in our barn so I could bring Igor home from the hospital. Michael and I went up in the loft of the barn to see how things were going. They were trying to seal a door on top shut so it wouldn't let all the cold winter air into our apartment. We had some insulation stored in another building on the property, where we were planning to build a house. Consequently, I took two of the workers there to show them where it was, so they could use it for our apartment. Michael wanted to stay down with the workers in the barn. Like any young boy he was interested in what they were doing, with all the noisy tools and interesting happenings with a jackhammer. God was protecting him from seeing something that could have traumatized him for a long time.

Two workers and I went up a ladder through a hole in the second story floor where the insulation was stored. Before we went back down the ladder, I asked one of the workers to help me put a piece of plywood up against the wall to cover a big opening where the wind was constantly blowing the insulation out. The other worker came over to take the sheet of plywood, thinking he was helping me. When I handed it to him, I became distracted and took one step back and I stepped into the air. I fell through a hole in the floor when I underestimated its location. I fell backwards 4 ½ meters (14 ½ ft.) down onto a concrete floor. I do not remember hitting the floor, due to a severe head injury. I was knocked out, which was a blessing, because I would have not been able to handle the pain. Some months later while I was recovering, I asked the Lord, "Where were you, I thought you protected me?" He said, *"I was right there with you, you are alive today because I was with you."* Later the Lord gave me a vision of myself lying on the ground and angels were holding my spirit in the air looking down at my body, to keep me from the pain. I did not feel pain until the ambulance came to pick me up. I was taken to a nearby hospital and put in a room full of people, and only remember having a lot of trouble breathing. Later I found out I had multiple broken ribs and my lung was punctured and filled with blood, which would explain the labored breathing. I had multiple broken bones: two crushed vertebrae, three breaks in my collar bone, a broken ankle, finger, sternum, nine breaks in my ribs, and my head needed many stitches. I had a bone graft, metal plates and screws put in my back, a pin put in my shoulder, and a cast on my ankle. When I awoke, I found myself in ICU in the same hospital that Igor had been in for his surgery.

How could this possibly be happening after only two and a half months since Igor's accident? It was clearly an attempt of the enemy to get rid of us both, but God is in control and will always protect us from the devil's plans. The days that followed my accident are a blur in so many ways with just bits and pieces of memory of my stay in ICU for ten days. Remember, the Holy Spirit told me to buy health insurance; the accident happened ten days after I purchased it, and I was dismissed from the hospital exactly when it ended. I was asked to leave the hospital after ten days in ICU, because the hospitals in Slovakia went bankrupt because of all the financial problems in the country post-communism. I had no therapy, except one lesson on getting in the wheelchair to go to the bathroom and how to stand up on the crutches and to put on the back brace I had to wear for months. My healing was totally based on prayer from around the world and God's answers. The Holy Spirit instructed me daily to rehab myself at home. Each day I decided to do something I could not do, such as stand up, take one step, feed myself, go to the bathroom;

slowly I was walking more and sitting up to eat, going to the bathroom on my own. I discovered that I had lost my sense of smell from the head injury when my friend apologized for the smells from the kitchen coming in my room. I said I didn't smell anything. She then went to the bathroom and got a bottle of perfume that was very strong and put it up to my nose and I smelled nothing. God turns bad things into good for His purpose. Because of this, I have been blessed to be able to go minister in the streets and in very unclean places like India and not be bothered by the smells. I decided to find the good in the situation rather than focus on the damage that was done.

In all our trials we continued to believe God's word, prayed daily, and read and listened to His Word. It was healing us both inside and out.

After a month at my friend's house, our apartment at Tri Duby was finished and it was time to take Igor out of the hospital and go home. Seven people came in two cars to get us. I remember going to his room in a wheelchair, after not seeing him for over a month, to get him to go home. It was right before Christmas, so it was a very exciting Christmas, even though we were both pretty helpless.

We went home to our little apartment with our beds in the living/dining room where the wood stove was placed to keep us warm. My sister and husband came to stay with us for a while to see that we were cared for. It was a true blessing and adventure for sure, especially when in the cold ice and snow the mice decided to come inside and make their home in the warmth with us. They were jumping on our bed, in my sister's sleeping bag; it was a funny but disturbing thing not knowing if a bouncy little critter would be jumping across your head at night. Then the water pipes froze, and we didn't have water and of course the holidays made it impossible for them to be fixed.

There were many other interesting adventures during our year-long healing process, like the Romanian man that came to take care of us in the beginning. He was instructed to cook for us, clean house, wash clothes, do shopping, and clean Igor, who was still not able to do much for himself. Our Romanian caregiver didn't think it was unusual to stay up all night singing, with the radio blasting and cooking in the kitchen, which kept us awake all night. One day I went to the doctor, and our helper was instructed to bathe Igor and get him dressed. Instead, when I came home, he was outside washing his car in the snow with his shirt off singing an opera, while Igor was in the house trying to fix the fire in the woodstove himself and burned holes in the new carpet with hot coals and was still in his dirty clothes. Needless to say, he was asked to leave shortly after.

God replaced him with a young couple that was exceptional at taking care of all our needs, for over a year. They did our shopping, took us to doctor's appointments, brought us water when the pipes froze, helped us keep the wood pile stocked, did our laundry, you name it, they did it. We really became like part of their family. An amazing couple that also they took care of eight orphan children and two of their own, of which one was handicapped. I will always be so grateful for all their help and the brothers and sisters in our church in Slovakia, family and friends in Slovakia and the United States that donated financially and prayed for our healing. We were definitely in the hands of Almighty God.

We had many more trials in our healing process, some that were even worse than the accidents, but I try to focus on the funny little episodes, as when during the night Igor fell into the woodpile trying to go to the bathroom in the dark. I certainly couldn't help him get up. I just tried to verbally instruct him how to get up and somehow, by the grace of God, he made it up in the wheelchair. It must have been very entertaining to our guardian angels, watching us go through all these things as incapable human beings. Igor took out the corner of the doorways with his wheelchair, which left plaster on the floor and a pretty ugly wall. Funny thing, he never noticed. Remember he was recovering from a coma. His food had to be put in a blender, he had to learn how to swallow again, to walk, to dress, bathe himself, like a child learning all over again. His body was so emaciated; he looked like he just came out of a concentration camp. I, on the other hand, looked like a bionic woman that just came out of a warzone, with metal around my body, in my body, on crutches, with a cast and bruises. I was a virtual mess.

Speaking of virtual, there was no such thing; we communicated through email by typing a letter on a disk with a word processor, then gave it to a young man at church and he sent it to whomever we wanted to contact and received our answer back on a disk as well. We had no TV, no phone (until a little later), only a tape player and a lot of tapes with Bible teachings, so our day was spent in prayer, listening to the Bible teachings, and reading the Bible for over one year as we slowly healed. I guess you could say we were in a monastery or in Bible College. It was all preparation for what God had called us to do. Every pain, every struggle would prove to be a very important part of our training for future ministry.

The Lord was with us through it all and He gave me many signs. He provided for us during such terrible trials and every day He sent an angel to watch over me. While in ICU, I saw an angel floating up by the ceiling of my room. It was like a flowing silver light in the form of an angel, long, curly, flowing hair, just watching over me. I asked one of the nurses at one point to give me a pencil and paper, so I could draw a picture of it, but my hand wasn't able to draw well at that time.

During this time, Igor was still in the infection hospital across town and had no idea what happened to me. Only that his mother told him I broke my arm. One day, while I was looking at the angel a man's face appeared next to it and he said, "I am with you and I am with Igor." Then he disappeared as quickly as he came. I am positive it was Jesus, because He promises in His Word that He never leaves us or forsakes us. I am sure He stayed with us both all through this very difficult trial. Some people might say she was just on drugs, but the truth is I asked them to stop all pain pills because I cannot tolerate them, so they gave me Tylenol and I didn't even take that. They didn't know it, but I used to hide it under my covers.

Igor and I are both walking miracles with a testament of God's miraculous healing power and answer to many prayers said for us. I am so thankful for all my family and friends that prayed for us, who came to stay with us, and gave financially to help us during this horrific trial.

I learned a very important lesson in all this: trust in the Lord always, ask others to pray for you, and be under a spiritual covering of a church and strong leaders that stand with you, especially when you are in strange lands where you are taking back territory for the Lord. Stay alert to the plans of the Enemy, and never give him a foothold or an open door with sin. Be wise as a serpent and gentle as a dove, pray without ceasing, especially in the Spirit. God is sovereign and loves us like no other. He will never forsake us nor leave us. His word is truth and will cancel every lie of the enemy in our mind.

He healed me, He set me free, He called me, He sent me, and He sanctified me for His glory.

-27-

GOD FINISHES WHAT HE STARTS

After coming back to America in the year 2000, I landed in Houston, Texas. I came with only one hundred dollars, a backpack with three changes of clothes, and a hope of returning with my son that came back to America with my daughter during my hospitalization. It didn't turn out the way I had planned, but God had a better plan. I was forced to stay in a shelter for a while that called itself Christian, but was far from it. While there, I began a prayer group on the weekends, when the management changed to a praying woman. I led all my three roommates to the Lord, was used abused and tormented while I was there, but God gave me a job with a Christian music company and moved me out after a month. I moved close to my job with the kindness of my boss and her husband until Igor came to America to be with me. Shortly after he came, the house across the street from where I worked came up for rent. We got it, miraculously, and we didn't have a car so it was very convenient. My boss took me to her church, which is still my home church today. Lindale Assembly of God has been my home, family away from home, and place of refuge, strength, help, hope, and love for twenty-three years now. I am forever grateful for my pastors Randy and Jana Meeks, Lyle and Lisa Countryman, and so many brothers and sisters that have helped us along the way and prayed us through many more trials.

In the beginning we had no furniture, so people from the church gave us a chair, a bed, and some dishes. Igor made a table for us out of some wood he found on the street; chairs came and slowly we made our house a home. We are so blessed. Whether we have a little or a lot, we are blessed!

One night when I lay down to sleep, I closed my eyes and had a vision. I saw a large tent that seemed to move from one spot to another. Then I heard the words, "I want you to start a ministry called A Cup of Cold Water." I was amazed by what I had just seen and heard, so I jumped up out of bed immediately and told Igor what just happened. We both prayed and asked God to reveal to us what that meant. I thought it meant to do evangelization with a tent. We were already doing evangelizations with a brother from church, so I shared my heart for this with him and he sort of tried to help me get it started but there just wasn't any fire or passion in it from him, so I finally just gave up on that idea.

In the meantime, I took the steps to establish the ministry legally as a corporation with the state. The very day I faxed the papers to the state for A Cup of Cold Water Ministries, Inc., my boss called me into his office and laid me off. I was both happy and sad, because now we had no income, but I felt the Lord was confirming I should go into fulltime ministry. He had already given me a full scholarship to Bible college to get my bachelor's degree in church ministry, so here was another step of faith to take.

Remember our inheritance, that we almost lost our lives over? It was part of the plan for this ministry to begin. We had no income, but we did have property in Slovakia. God began to move on the hearts of people to buy property. Our real estate agent began to email us about a prospective buyer and we began to negotiate for the sale of part of the land at Tri Duby. After many back-and-forth emails, we negotiated the price which came just in time to cover all our needs and the plans God had for our lives in the ministry. We had prayed for the land to be used by God for ministry in Slovakia, but God had a different way. He would use it for ministry to multiple nations. Slovakia is still in my heart to go and share the gospel.

Before these negotiations, while I was still working, the house we were renting at the time was now asking us to leave because the landlord was going to move back in. We started to look at places to live, but did not see anything we liked or could afford. Actually, we couldn't afford anything or qualify for anything, but God opened a way for us supernaturally. We found a house perfect in every way for us, right across the street from our church, close to my job, but we had no down payment or way to hold the house by making a contract on it. At the same time, I received a credit card application in the mail with blank checks. We prayed and God confirmed to us through His word to go to the promised land and buy the house, strictly on faith. We went to the realtor and gave them a $500 check from the credit card, and they said they had another buyer, but they would submit our bid and see what happened. A few days later we got the call, it was ours! We were excited but concerned, because we didn't have anything in our account but a few dollars. Igor called his mom and told her about the house and the amount of money we needed for the closing costs, which we would need in a few weeks and she responded, "That is very nice, but where are you going to get it?" He asked if she could help, but no response. Much to our surprise as the closing was only a few days away, we saw our bank account contained the exact amount we needed to go to the closing. She had given us the money after all. Oh, the other miracle was that we qualified for the loan over the phone and showed no paper work to anyone, thanks to the mortgage disaster plans that were happening at that time. God uses everything for our favor. We marched into the closing to get our new house with our check, and walked out with a check for $1900, because they lowered our interest rate and we didn't have to pay what we were supposed to. That worked out nice, since we needed to buy beds and some other furniture. God is so good.

That was just the beginning of blessings. Back to the sale of our land, yes it went through and allowed us to pay off the mortgage of our house after three months of payments, and we were able to buy a one-year-old car with only 4,000 miles. After driving it for fifteen years and 326,000 miles, we finally bought a new used car with cash. Don't ever think that God can't supply all your needs.

In 2005, I received a phone call from my dear friend and fellow minister Pablo Cerna, asking me to come to Honduras to preach at a crusade. I said, "What, I can't speak Spanish and I don't have a clue how to preach at a crusade." After weeks of praying and waiting to hear from God about going, I heard, "Go." What happened after that was one miracle after another.

We built our first church there after we preached under a mango tree to forty people and they came to my husband and asked if we would build them a church. We had the ground breaking ceremony a year later. To date, we have built four A Cup of Cold Water churches and helped to build eleven other churches in Honduras, and have plans for more. We have also built a school for education and job training, a free clinic, established a children's feeding program for 160 children, and built 29 homes for the homeless and rebuilt many other homes.

Recently, in 2020, we experienced two category 4 hurricanes within two weeks of each other and our ministry suffered many loses. My son and his wife lost their home along with thousands of others. Three of our churches suffered loss, and all of the people in the area lost their homes. It took us several years to recover, but the people are resilient, hardworking, and rebuilt again. I was there during the floods and experienced a lot of trauma along with most everyone there. God miraculously saved us and all our loved ones there and is faithful to restore what was lost.

God took us from Honduras to El Salvador, and we have built a church there and feed children and the elderly every month with the help of a strong woman of God, Pastor Marta. In 2020 we started our second church in San Salvador that is growing weekly. Our vision is to build a place for them to meet soon. We have also supported a men's rehab center in San Salvador where men are set free from addictions. Men come there from prison and the streets and are given an opportunity to receive Jesus and be transformed by His love and grace. We have also helped to build and finish four churches and purchased land to build two more in Mexico, a school and church in Zambia, and every month we feed six pastors in Cuba. They are without enough money to even feed their families. They are so very grateful it is such a joy to help them. Along with that we have purchased property there to begin a church that will mainly minister to children with the help of a pastor we have sent to bring the gospel to the people. After he came home, he received a phone call during the night with this amazing testimony. God saved a woman and her children who were fishing in the ocean for their livelihood when suddenly the innertube they were floating in began to deflate. None could swim, the mom and her two small children began to pray and ask God to save them. As they opened their eyes, they found themselves on the shore completely safe. God is still a miracle working God. Consequently, it has begun a revival there.

Because of the danger for the people we are associated with in certain areas of the world, I will not state the places, but only say that God can open doors that no man can shut and He took us to South Asia to two different nations to build churches and feed orphans. Our ministry has been established in one nation, and we have a church, orphanage with twenty-eight orphans, and wonderful pastors and leaders that help train forty pastors in remote mountainous areas. We also help to feed these pastors. They also have a sewing ministry where women of a different faith are learning a trade and also receiving Jesus Christ as their Savior. Transformation is the word that always comes to my mind when I think of what Jesus does. It has been the most exciting and fulfilling life, and as you have seen, not without trials.

To date we have been missionaries to America, Slovakia, Honduras, El Salvador, South Asia, South Korea, and The Philippines and still pray, "Here I am Lord, send me." And He is still speaking to me about going to more nations. Where else can we go Lord; send us.

My ministry did not begin until the age of forty-six; I am now seventy-five, and God is still sending me. Don't give up on your calling; it is so worth it, even with all the trials and tests, pains and sorrows, good times and bad times. He is faithful to fulfill what He has promised. If you have a word from God and haven't seen it happen yet, hold on to it, pray and believe in the vision, pursue your destiny, and God will empower you with His Spirit to fulfill it.

We have seen the hand of God in our lives like we could have never imagined. The Lord is gracious and merciful to His children; His children do not have to beg for bread, He will supply all their need according to His riches in glory by Christ Jesus (Phil. 4:19).

A Cup of Cold Water Ministries began in 2004 after going through the worst trials of our lives. The birthing process can be painful and difficult, but when the vision is born, it is glorious to see all that God has done. God is so good and we desire to share His goodness, mercy, and love wherever we can to fulfill the great commission.

"Go therefore and make disciples of all the nations,
baptizing them in the name of the Father and of the
Son and of the Holy Spirit" (Matt. 28:19NKJV).

If you feel like you will never reach your vision or the calling in your life, do not despise small beginnings, you have no idea what God can lead you to that might be bigger than you can even imagine. As you can see with our story, it did not happen easily, yet God was with us through it all.

We are not special; just ordinary people. Not qualified, not young, not with lots of credentials, but lots of Jesus and everything is possible with Him.

If you haven't accepted Jesus Christ as your Savior, now is your opportunity.

Let us pray:

Father, I come to you with sorrow in my heart because I am a sinner. Thank you that you sent your Son, Jesus, to die for all my sins. Forgive me Lord and wash me of all my past and give me a new life in You Jesus. I believe that you died for my sins and now you are seated at the right hand of the Father and are interceding for me. I give all of myself to You today, Jesus, and trust that You will guide me and empower me with the Holy Spirit to serve You and live for You all the days of my life. Take me Lord, mold me, and make me more like You every day. In Jesus name I pray. Amen.

If you have sincerely believed and decided to follow Jesus in your life, then your life is no longer your own. It belongs to Him. Give all of yourself to Him, every day, read the Bible, pray, worship, and seek Him with all your heart, soul, and mind. He has great things planned for your life, and He is waiting with open arms to walk with you through this life. We would love to hear from you and pray for you; please contact us on Facebook at A Cup of Cold Water Ministries, Inc. @acupofcoldwater or let us know at our website: www.acupofcoldwatermissions.org.

about the author

Linda Demjen is a missionary with a burning desire to share her story and life truths with others. Her exciting journey started in 1991 and continues today. After a vision in 2005, she and her husband founded A Cup of Cold Water Ministries, Inc. Her commitment to the call has afforded her the privilege to serve in many nations and prosper the kingdom of God wherever God sends her.

Linda received a Bachelor's Degree in Church Ministry and Ministry license from The Sure Foundation Theological Institute in 2007. She has served in her local church for 23 years in many areas as a Bible teacher, prayer leader, deacon, teen ministry sponsor, small group leader, and missions coordinator.

Her passion since becoming a Christian has been to reach the lost and serve the poor and disadvantaged. She has served as a missionary and minister in North and Central America, Eastern Europe, Mexico, and South Asia. Her ministry has reached thousands for Christ and provided education, church and school buildings, feeding programs, medical care, and housing for the poor.

When Linda is not on a mission trip, she spends time with her family and her dog, Lucy. It is probably her if you see a white-haired grandmother struggling to go down a slide at the park in Houston with the prompting of her three-year-old grandson. Her grandchildren have a big place in her heart. She says they help her to stay young. Her family makes her life complete.

www.ingramcontent.com/pod-product-compliance
Lightning Source LLC
Chambersburg PA
CBHW020246130626
46549CB00005B/2081